5/4

THE HAIRCURL PAPERS

and other searches for the lost individual

Books by William K. Zinsser:

ANY OLD PLACE WITH YOU

SEEN ANY GOOD MOVIES LATELY?

THE CITY DWELLERS

WEEKEND GUESTS

THE HAIRCURL PAPERS

THE
HAIRCURL
PAPERS

and other searches

for the lost individual

William K. Zinsser

HARPER & ROW, PUBLISHERS

New York, Evanston, and London

Many of the chapters in this book first appeared, often in somewhat different form, in the following magazines, and are reprinted here by permission: *Life:* "The Haircurl Papers." *The Saturday Evening Post:* "Verel Modacrylic and Mr. Inside Floormat"; "Don't Look Now." *Horizon:* "Encode Me, My Sweet Encodable You"; "A Little Flight Music"; "What Ever Happened to Privacy?"; "Far Out on Long Island"; "Is It True What the Movies Say About . . . ?"; "The Vanishing Boffola"; "Will Nobody Bid Any More?" *Esquire:* "There Are Smiles." *Harper's:* "Harold Arlen." *Playboy:* "Saltpeter and the Wolf." *Glamour:* "Confessions of a Celluloid Eater." *Show Business Illustrated:* "Nobody Here But Us Sheep." *The New York Herald Tribune:* "Dig We Must."

FIRST EDITION

LIBRARY OF CONGRESS CATALOG CARD NUMBER: 64:12684

C-O

CONTENTS

For

AMY FRASER ZINSSER

With love and gratitude

Preface

There is a moderately famous painting called "The Vanishing American," which shows a lone American Indian in the middle of the vast country that he once dominated and then lost. Today it is not necessary to be an Indian to be a vanishing American. Millions of us are disappearing into a bland and blurry realm where we renounce the very qualities which, as the old movie cliché goes, made America strong: individuality, humor and a lively sense of protest. Where once we had the fiber to want to be ourselves, we now want to be like everybody else, and will gladly submit to any masseur who finds it useful to knead us into that shapeless state.

Encoded by the banks, zipcoded by the post office and digited by the telephone company, we have been reduced to numerals by most of the organizations that govern our affairs. We are mesmerized by the vacant smile of the airline stewardess and trapped by the movies that she shows in mid-flight. We allow our privacy to be invaded as never before, and without a whimper. We won't even walk out on a bad play. Our women and girls look alike because they have all been told to put curlers in their hair—and, presumably, never to take them out. Our magazines look alike because we will uncomplainingly read the same article over and over again, especially if it's a probe of America's sexual "revolution," masquerading in the robes of sociological jargon, or a study in depth of a movie "personality" who has no depth—or personality.

We buy expensive household items that we don't need —egg-openers and cordless electric carving sets—because the catalogue dazzles us with verbiage which, ostensibly in English, means nothing. At auctions we purchase objects of art for status or profit rather than for love, relying on our decorator to tell us which King George is "in," and on our accountant to tell us if Matisse gives us a better tax break than Ming. The decorator even rules our choice of motorboat; its curtains and valances are now more important than its engine, for we must run no risk of leaving our certified "image" back on land when we rough it for a few hours at sea. And speaking of images, the dread vision of saltpeter continues to tap at the window and to hold the entire younger generation in its chilly grip.

These are some of the lost individuals—and lost values— that this book has gone in search of. We need dissenters, mavericks and wits again to jolt us out of our sheepish condition. Today very few groups are formed on the basis of good old-fashioned outrage, like the Anti-Digit Dialing League, the Committee Against Obnoxious Commercials, and the Committee to Keep New York Habitable, nor do many individuals continue to keep the watch. As a resident of New York State I salute E. Kenneth Froslid, who single-handed won for us the legal right not to have "World's Fair" on our 1964 license plates, his reason being that the Fair isn't a state project but a private corporation which we are not required to advertise. These are the true vigilantes of modern America, and they are fighting a lonely battle.

The real quest of this book is for originality, in one form or another, which explains the presence here of Harold Arlen and a scattering of other people who have given me pleasure with the freshness of their work. I wanted them along on the ride. For the vanishing American has also lost the courage of his addictions. He plays it safe. He reads books chosen for him by book clubs, watches TV programs chosen for him by a rating machine, see plays chosen for production because they can be pre-sold to theater parties. We will only get originality if we demand it—and if we proclaim our likes as strongly as our dislikes. Joy is as important as anger to the lost individual who wants to be saved. With them both he has a good chance, unlike the Indian, of getting his country back.

New York
February 1, 1964

1. *Encode Me,*
My Sweet Encodable You

By ⑈0⁅⑅0ᵐᵐ000⁅⑈ 030ᵐᵐ⑂ᵐᵐ0⑂8⑂⑂5ᵐᵐᵒ

THAT'S MY NAME UP THERE AT THE TOP
of this page, and I want to say right away what a thrill it
is to see it in print. There's nothing like a by-line to give
someone a sense of his own identity.

Actually that isn't the name I was born with. My legal
name is William K. Zinsser. My family gave it to me, and I
think that was very nice of them. But ⑈0⁅⑂0ᵐᵐ000⁅⑈
030ᵐᵐ⑂ᵐᵐ0⑂8⑂⑂5ᵐᵒ is my new name, given to me by the
Chase Manhattan Bank just last year. The bank went to a
lot of trouble to think it up and to make it different
from anybody else's. Believe it or not, there isn't another

1

⑆021000021⑆ 030⑈1⑉0181150⑈ in the whole world, and that's a mighty big thing to be able to say.

My new name isn't an easy one to catch at first. I'll admit that. Sometimes I look at it on my checks, where the bank has so kindly imprinted it in magnetic ink, and I think "Is that really me?" and then I realize that it really is. The bank assures me that it has a machine which can read my name "with incredible speed and accuracy."

What an assurance that is! In this age of exploding populations, when everybody has been divorced two or three times and nobody knows who *any*body is, I have a friend at Chase Manhattan who can read my name as easy as John Doe. (Maybe easier—John Doe is one of those names that I never can get straight.) The fact that my friend is a machine, that the personal element has gone out of banking, ought to bother me. But then I stop to think how much pleasure I give my new metal friend at the bank.

See how his 200-watt eyes blink with joy as he runs his sensitized tongue over my magnetized checks and realizes that it is ME, his old buddy. See the incredible speed and accuracy with which he taps out—for whatever human employees may be left at my branch—the two words that they need to know: ZINSSER and OVERDRAWN. See how the vice-presidents join hands and dance around the faithful computer, giving him fraternal jabs on the shoulder, showering him with praise. "What speed!" says one. "What accuracy!" says another. "Incredible!" says a third. It is such vignettes as this that make modern America a dynamic place to live. I wouldn't exchange it for all the magnetic ink in China.

I'll confess that I resisted the shift to electronic banking at first. That was well over a year ago, when the bank sent me several hundred checks in a new format with my new name printed on them, and ordered me to start using them right away. I hated them thoroughly. The old checks were handsome in design, and they almost made check-writing enjoyable. The new checks were meanly designed and ugly, and my new name, splayed across the bottom like a cryptogram, jumped out to insult anyone who cares for the English language, or at least for the Western alphabet.

What annoyed me most, however, were the directives that accompanied the new checks. They were awash in self-congratulation over the electronic feat. Now, boasted the bank, it would be able to serve me better, give me more efficient treatment, process my checks faster. But I have no complaint with the way the bank has been serving me up to now. If anything, I want a bank that will process my checks slower and give me more time to cover them.

Banks may have many defects, but slowness is not one. An electronic computer will need to move with the speed of light to outrace an old-fashioned human banker in asking for interest due, or demanding extra collateral on a loan when the stock market drops. Obviously the bank had decided to install an electronic system for its *own* convenience but was trying to persuade me that it was really for *my* convenience.

Such tactics cried out for counterattack. I hurried to my bank and, by cleverly applying to different tellers, obtained enough of the old-fashioned checks to last a year. It was the happiest check-writing year of my life, made all the more pleasant by the testy notes that I kept receiving from the bank as the year wore on.

"Our records show," the notes said, "that you are not now using your encoded checks." (This at least proved that real people were still keeping records over there.) "If you have a supply of checks printed in magnetic ink but have not started using them, please commence using these checks and destroy all un-encoded checks you may have."

I couldn't commence using the new checks because I had thrown them away the day they arrived. I went on flooding the bank with old ones. I was a man possessed, or at least not un-enpossessed. There are not many pleasures left to the individual in this organized society, but one of them is to use un-encoded checks when the Chase Manhattan Bank is trying to encode you.

One day, of course, the old checks ran out and I had to surrender. Since then I've grown accustomed to my new name, possibly because it is turning up on other forms besides my checks. A while ago I received several hundred deposit slips with my encoded name printed on them.

"Please use these tickets for every deposit you make," said the accompanying note. "Your cooperation will insure accuracy in maintaining your account." Again, I don't think it's up to *me* to insure the bank's accuracy—that's what insurance companies are for—but the bank was insistent: "It's a good idea to keep a supply of deposit tickets handy wherever you might be—at home, at your office, in your car. Two or three tickets in your wallet or pocketbook will provide added insurance."

It is nice to know the three places where the Chase Manhattan Bank thinks I am most likely to be. Its list shows a touching belief in the American verities. (It's also nice to know what the Chase Manhattan Bank thinks is "a good idea.") But there are several other places where I might just be instead, such as the ballpark or the bar, especially if they keep hounding me, and I have no intention of carrying encoded deposit tickets all over New York just to provide added insurance for the biggest bank in the world. If I feel like walking into my bank and depositing some money on an ordinary slip, I'm going to do it. There are limits beyond which I will not be enpushed.

After all, I've got to preserve *some* individuality. Any

month now the telephone company is going to take away my phone exchange—lovable old YU 8—and give me a seven-digit number that is all my own, unlike any other number in the country, which some machine will learn with incredible speed and accuracy, even if nobody else does, and that shift is *really* going to be hard to fight. At our summer house I have already been given a number so dreary—516-288-2895—that I doze off while telling my friends what it is, and the post office has given me two zip codes, 11978 and 10028, which I have no intention of remembering. In fact, I have no intention of using anybody's zip code.

The phone company and the bank have been taking a lot of ads to tell us what a tremendous favor they are doing by giving us all a number. The post office is also very pleased with itself for giving us such swell zip codes, which will "insure faster, more efficient service." Honestly, the kindness of these big organizations is enough to melt the heart.

2. Verel Modacrylic
and Mr. Inside Floormat

WRITERS WHO PONDER THE FOLLIES OF modern America—and the journalistic woods have never been so full of folly-ponderers—love to imagine an archaeologist of the future coming upon our ruins. "What would he make of *that?*" they ask, citing some artifact like a jukebox, and there they rest their case, certain that the archaeologist would be stumped. My only complaint with this approach is that it is projected too far ahead. America is full of objects that I don't understand right now.

They are objects which I never knew existed and which serve functions that I never dreamed were necessary. Seeing them in advertisements, I am as bewildered in 1964 as any archaeologist will be in 2964. To some extent my trouble is linguistic, for the idiom that describes these items is as strange as the items themselves. It is a language shorn of syntax and strewn with words like "leatherette," which make me uneasy, for I have no idea what they mean and have no way of finding out.

"Leatherette" at least contains one genuine noun, and that's a help. But some words don't even offer that comfort. Consider the word "superette." It consists of a prefix meaning "big" and a suffix meaning "small"—and nothing else. Try that one on your Rosetta Stone, Mr. Future Archaeologist. If there's anyone in the present audience who doesn't know what a superette is, it's a little supermarket. And if you wonder how a market that's big can also be small, you're beginning to understand my problem and are ready for the main course.

The main course has as its textbook the catalogue of Hammacher Schlemmer, a housewares store in Manhattan which took a two-page ad in the "New York Times" for its custom-fitted bomb shelter, complete with $249 TV set. Within this one catalogue, which arrives periodically, I find compressed almost everything that baffles me, both in merchandise and terminology, about the society that I allegedly live in. So profuse are the examples that I hardly know where to begin, but I'll start with the "Select-a-Rest," a $439 couch which "electrically raises legs or back in varying degrees at touch of button; for personal support."

The Select-a-Rest typifies the emphasis on ease that is the catalogue's pervading theme. These are, on the whole, objects designed to soften tasks that are not arduous in the first place: an electric pencil sharpener for $29.95 ("just insert pencil"), a cordless electric carving set for $19.95, a push-button shine for $29.95 ("tap button with toe;

place shoe against bonnet"), an egg scissors for $5.95 to open a boiled egg. I'm no student of the economy, least of all my own, but if that many people are willing to shell out thirty clams for an electric pencil sharpener ("simply shell out clams")—so many that a manufacturer finds it worthwhile to make them—there is either nothing wrong with the economy or something wrong with the people.

As for the $439 to get "personal support" from Select-a-Rest, that's a lot of personal support. Which brings up another linguistic riddle: what is personal support? Does it differ from impersonal support? Does it mean that if I buy Select-a-Rest it will support me personally but not my friends? Perhaps it will support my personal friends—a breed so often mentioned in the phrase "he's a personal friend of mine"—but not my animal friends.

This is one of modern America's most puzzling words—and not merely because it has spawned the peculiar sub-adjective "personalized." I often notice that an actress, stricken during the run of a play, has called in her "personal physician." What other kind is there? If the medical schools ever turn out an impersonal physician, one who will keep his hands off the patient and look away during an examination, he will be the most sought-after doctor in the land.

Speaking of personal friends, you can get a "guest closet kit" at Hammacher Schlemmer for $175. This doesn't seem to include the guest, but it does include twenty-seven squares of Plushtile and many "color coordinated materials." Plushtile is described as "55% Acrilan Acrylic, 45% Verel Modacrylic on an interlocking back; can be lifted out to change pattern, clean, even move with you. Color-fast, long-wearing, non-matting, non-allergenic. In 20 decorator colors."

Curiously, I don't happen to know what Acrilan Acrylic and Verel Modacrylic are, but I don't doubt for a minute that they can move with me. If I ever left them behind in the guest closet, they would probably come running out and jump in the car. I do know, however, what the twenty decorator colors are. They are the colors that decorators come in: ruddy, flushed, wine red, Fire Island tan, sun lamp, sunburn pink, Noxzema, pancake, talc, office yellow, ashen, white, ulcer gray, subway green, soot, toast, English muffin, five o'clock shadow, midnight and winter blue. I have met decorators in all these colors, though not many of them were long-wearing and some weren't even color-fast.

This is another construction—the noun-adjective like "decorator"—that will vex the archaeologists. Tricky as Linear B, it leaves the scholar to guess the meaning out of various possibilities, none of them plausible. A bathroom scale in the Hammacher Schlemmer catalogue, for example, is "doctor-type for no stooping." Does this mean that the scale looks like a doctor or is somehow shaped like a doctor? Does it mean that doctors don't stoop? I could swear that I've seen doctors stoop.

Then again I couldn't really swear to anything. The catalogue addles me. I see an item like "wood snack table set" and my head spins. Is it a table for eating wood snacks? What about the D-Frost Master which "ends hand defrosting"? But I haven't *been* defrosting my hands. Ought I to pay $79.95 for a "floor hair dryer," which presumably dries hair that has fallen on the floor? What is a "hostess towel tree"—a towel tree hung with hostesses? How can I rest easy on the $219 Barcalounger ("for relaxation, comfort, TV viewing") when I see that its pillow back is made of Premier Naugahyde? Surely Premier Naugahyde was defenestrated in the Bosnian coup of 1912?

Confronted with such an abstract language, I lose my grip on reality. And language is only part of the problem.

Equally unreal are the concepts that it expresses, such as this one: "Waterford Cut Plexiglas has old world charm but in virtually unbreakable Plexiglas; a practical version of crystal."

The sentence is positively electrical in its balance of positive and negative currents. Every clause carries its immediate cancellation. The whole point of Waterford glass is that it is not Plexiglas; old world charm derives from the fact that an object is both old and breakable; and part of the enjoyment of crystal is the awareness that it is not practical.

A more perfect conundrum could hardly be posed by a wizard in Wonderland or Oz. And yet it is no isolated case. Modern America loves authentic names but hates the authentic flaws that accompany them, so it labors to root them out. "Mr. Inside Floormat," for instance, is available at Hammacher Schlemmer in "green striped nylon tweed." This material is rather hard to picture, as it can't be both nylon and tweed.

Obviously tweed is in the floormat only as an idea. Everybody likes tweed coats; therefore they would like a tweed floormat. But tweed gets dirty and wears out and shouldn't be wet. So the solution is to make the tweed of nylon, and everyone is happy—everyone, that is, except the archaeologists of the future and a few thousand crofters in the Scottish Highlands.

A similar paradox lies in a stove described in the catalogue as follows: "Radiant Broiling with Quartz Foil gives charcoal flavor without charcoal ($69.95)." Here we see a circle so fully turned that it swallows itself. Charcoal flavor began as a by-product of early outdoor stoves. Nobody really wanted his steak to taste like charcoal, but as this was unavoidable we were told that it was a great flavor and to enjoy it. Now that outdoor ranges have improved and steaks can taste like steaks again, they don't seem authentic. Hence this broiler that adds a tinge of charcoal. In fact, it doesn't go far enough. The next model should char the steaks on the outside and fill the patio with smoke.

No thought is spared in Hammacher Schlemmer to make the living easy and beautiful. It's not merely that the crystal doesn't break because it isn't crystal. The air is good ("Dynamic Ionaire Mark VII provides negative ions to reduce dry, staleair effects; restores natural ion balance of air. $149.50"). The floors are clean ("Disposable boots of polyethelene film are for bad weather, avoiding dirt"). The lights don't have to be turned on or off (Homelighter does it automatically, "according to sunlight"; Time-All does, too—"and does it indefinitely until you change the cycle; misleads burglars").

No more need you eat leftovers ("Party Grill makes leftovers into bite-sized toasted sandwiches"). No more need you rest on a plain old-fashioned pillow ("Comfort Aid," an object that looks like a pillow but costs $29.95, is "for either head or foot elevation; use for relaxation, tension and pressure relief"). You don't even have to hold the telephone; simply fit your "executive phone stand" ($39.95) with a "transistorized phone amplifier ($34.95) for hands-free conference calls."

Comforts don't cease when you go for a drive. Your car can be a home-away-from-home if you get the Headrest that "attaches to auto seat for rests, naps." I had supposed that this nap-inducing cushion was meant only for passengers, but in an adjacent photograph the driver is also resting his head on one and is presumably well on his way to bye-bye land, if not eternity.

Another trait that the future archaeologist will note is our mania for decoration. As any dime-story browser knows, no object in America is too cheap to be embellished

with some sort of pattern, usually floral, and anyone foolish enough to want a plain object must search far and pay
more.

This point is also amply documented in Hammacher
Schlemmer's catalogue, especially in its bathroom, which
has a "poppy" shower curtain in Glo-chintz (the chintz
that isn't); a "poppy" tissue-box on "jade-white Plexiglas"
(since when has jade been white?); a "poppy" hamper,
"poppy" basket and "poppy" brush holder; four "poppy"
bath bottles; a hand-decorated "poppy" toilet seat; and a
"poppy" decorated scale. Now there's a bathroom with
poppies. The scale also comes in an undecorated model,
but that doesn't mean it is intended to stay undecorated,
if I understand correctly—and there's no reason why I
should—this sentence that describes it: "Slip own wall-
paper, paint color, curtain fabric sample under see-thru
lid to match decor."

Outside the bathroom there is also much to be embellished. You can get a "decorated toast cover with hand-
painted red bud roses," or a "decorated phone stand,
floral on white, which holds 2 books, all phones." (It's odd
that anyone would want all phones on one phone stand—
the upstairs phone, downstairs phone and kitchen phone—
but that's what decoration will do.) There are bottle
stoppers "imprinted with our gnomes"—maybe *that's* who
writes the catalogue—and there is a "guest terry robe with
choice of any 2-toned colored name or 3-letter monogram."

Thus even the guest must be decorated, perhaps to help
find him when he strays into the color-coordinated guest
closet. Of course this means inviting the same guest again
and again, or inviting guests who happen to have the same
name or initials. The worst thing would be for a guest
to drop in unexpectedly. He would be doomed to wear an
undecorated terry robe and would probably spend most of

the weekend, out of sheer insecurity, behind the poppy shower curtain.

And now if you'll excuse me, I'm going to put my head on my 6-Way Prop Pillow of lightweight polyfoam (if I can think of six ways to do it), take a drink from my Marbleized Rack Set (chairside size), put some wax-tipped Airfoam Nods in my ears and Sleep Shade on my eyes, clear the room of negative ions with dynamic Mark VII, turn on the Time-All to mislead burglars, and drop off for a few minutes. If the doorbell rings, it's probably the "Home Massager" that I ordered from Hammacher Schlemmer. As described in the catalogue, "Oster Stimulax, Jr., imparts the rotating, patting motions of Swedish massage." I understand that young Oster studied with his dad in Stockholm—old man Stimulax was an eminent masseur—and for my money ($32.95) I personally think he's going to give me a lot of personal relief. He's doctor-type.

3. The Haircurl Papers

A Selection of Recent Letters to the Editor Of "Haircurl" Magazine

DEAR "HAIRCURL":

I am fifteen and am considered pretty in my group. I wear baby-pink hair rollers, jumbo size. I have been going steady with a certain boy for 2½ years and he has never seen me without my rollers. The other night I took them off and we had a terrible fight. "Your head looks small," he told me. He called me a dwarf and said I had misled him. How can I win him back?

HEARTSICK,
Speonk, N.Y.

14

DEAR HEARTSICK:

You have only yourself to blame for doing something so stupid. The latest "Haircurl" survey shows that 94% of American girls now wear rollers in their hair 21.6 hours a day and 359 days a year. You tried to be different and you lost your fella. Take our advice and get some super-jumbo rollers (they come in your favorite baby-pink shade, too) and your head will look bigger than ever and twice as lovely. Don't ever take them off again and Mr. Right will be ringing your doorbell once more.

*

DEAR "HAIRCURL":

My problem is an intimate one, but I'm so upset that I just have to ask your advice.

My boy friend likes to run his fingers through my hair. The trouble is he keeps getting them pinched in my rollers. The other night a terribly embarrassing episode happened. We were at the movies and somehow my boy friend got two of his fingers caught (it was right where the medium roller meets the clip-curl) and couldn't get them out. I felt very conspicuous leaving the theater with his hand still in my hair, and going home on the bus several people gave us "funny looks." Fortunately I was able to reach my stylist at home and he came right over with his tools and got poor Jerry loose. Jerry was very mad and said he's not going to date me again until I get some rollers that don't have this particular habit. He said next time he might get his whole HAND caught. I think he is being unfair, but he "means business." Can you help me?

FRANTIC,
Buffalo

DEAR FRANTIC BUFFALO:

We're sorry to have to tell you that no rollers have yet been developed that do not occasionally catch the fingers of boys who tousle. The roller industry, however, is working very hard on the problem, as this complaint frequently comes up. Meanwhile why not ask Jerry to wear mittens? That way you'll be happy and he'll be safe.

*

DEAR "HAIRCURL":

I am seven years old. My mommy thinks I should get a straight body perm, but my stylist thinks I would look better in a pouf-do. What do *you* think?

BETTY J.,
Tarzana, Calif.

DEAR BETTY J.:

You have undoubtedly heard the expression "Mother knows best." Well, she doesn't. Parents just will go on being old-fashioned. Why, we get letters all the time complaining about mommies and daddies who don't want their daughter to get a perm until she is nine or even ten. How square can you get? We at "Haircurl" feel that every girl should be in curlers by age four. Which brings us—or did you guess it already?—to the answer to your question. Of course your stylist is right. Go, go, go and get that pouf-do!

*

DEAR "HAIRCURL":

Your last issue, with its special feature—"374 Different Comb-Outs by Mr. Ned of Coral Gables"—was one of the swellest editions of any magazine that I have ever seen, and in general the diagrams of roller positions were as easy as pie to follow. But I have run into a distressing problem in connection with Number 206, or "Cuddle Coif." The comb-out won't comb out!

I did everything just like you said, and it wasn't because I hurried. In fact, I never spend less than six hours a day on a do. I used twenty-three rollers of all sizes, set them on a bias, and added the forty-six back-turned clip-curls at the cheeks and in a row along the lower part of the head. Then I sprayed on the setting lotion. The kind I use is called Perma-Lac. Maybe I used too much. Now that I think back, I remember that it came out of the nozzle faster than I expected.

Anyway, I let it work and then went to my comb-out station to backbrush the setting out according to your instructions. I first suspected I was in trouble when I had difficulty removing the rollers and curlers. They were matted into the hair and it took me three and a half hours (longer than usual) to get them all out. I expected my hair to "fall into layered place," as you said it would. Instead it sprang back into roller position, JUST AS IF THE ROLLERS WERE STILL IN!

Nothing I do will make these rolls uncoil. They have the sticky texture of hard candy. Personally I do not find the style attractive, not to mention it is quite uncomfortable. When will my comb-out comb out? I have had it six weeks already and it shows no sign of loosening.

DISTRAUGHT,
Tulsa

DEAR DISTRAUGHT:

If we thought you could do without your head for a few days (ha, ha), we would ask you to send it in to our up-to-date laboratory, where qualified tonsorial engineers pre-test virtually all the settings that are published in "Haircurl." We say "virtually" because we can find no record of Number 206 being tested. We also find that Mr. Ned has moved from Coral Gables and left no forwarding address.

Frankly, your query has us "stumped"—and we don't stump easily. Only last week we were consulted on a serious problem of "seaweed hair," the straggly condition that afflicts so many women who spend their summers near the water. We suggested to the lady in question that she check her hair for actual seaweed, and sure enough she found fourteen large strands.

But this doesn't solve *your* complaint, does it? At our daily editorial conference we girls "put our heads together" and came up with two tips that might help you out of your jam (no pun intended). First, why not consult your family counselor? He can teach you how to adjust to your condition vis-à-vis your social environment. After several weeks of counseling you won't even notice that people are laughing at you, or, if you *do* still notice, you'll be able to laugh right back! If this treatment is not effective, we strongly recommend surgery. Modern doctors have instruments which can cut through the most agglutinated (gummy) substances formed by human chemistry. Your surgeon will know just what to do. The operation is a fairly common one.

*

DEAR "HAIRCURL":

I have a pretty collection of kerchiefs to wear over the curlers in my hair. I have a plastic kerchief for rainy days, several cotton kerchiefs in flowered patterns that "go nicely" with my yellow or salmon slacks for shopping downtown, an imitation silk kerchief for the office, a chiffon kerchief for evenings, a lovely lightweight mesh kerchief for the beach, etc., etc.

The reason I'm writing you is that my girl friend has asked me to be a bridesmaid in her wedding next month. What kind of kerchief would be proper over my curlers for this occasion?

BEWILDERED,
Boston

DEAR BEWILDERED:

Your kerchief should be the same color as your bridesmaid's dress and preferably of the same material. The bride will, of course, wear a white kerchief over her curlers, probably of peau de soie or organza (she may also want to attach a sprig of stephanotis), so you should not wear white, too. Remember, this is "her" day.

*

DEAR "HAIRCURL":

I am nineteen and was voted "most chic gal" in my sorority. But this week my colorist and I had a little tiff and now I'm all confused.

I have a favorite dress which is of apricot. (I mean the color is apricot; it is not made of apricot.) The jacket is violet, figured with beige, puce, aqua, emerald and taupe. The bag and shoes are café-au-lait, and the hat and gloves are putty. I feel that my hair should be rust to "pick up" the apricot dress.

My colorist says that the height of fashion is restraint. He suggests a coal-black hairdo tastefully flecked with green and with a very simple blond streak down the center which will "pick up" both the café-au-lait and the putty. Is he right? I know I have good taste in clothes, but I don't want to goof it all with the wrong hair tint.

Yours truly,
PATTY M.,
Kalamazoo

DEAR PATTY:

Maybe your colorist meant that the bag and shoes should be tinted black and that the hat and gloves should be flecked with green and have a blond streak. He sounds like a really good colorist, and that *would* be a fun combination. We're assuming that you'd accent the whole outfit with some gay jewelry. Have you thought of a long string of those bright Guatemalan beads? Heavenly!

It's good for a girl and her colorist to have a little tiff now and then. You both have integrity and you both have swell ideas. Don't be afraid to thrash your ideas out, even if you come to blows. Most girls are bigger than their colorist anyway.

*

DEAR "HAIRCURL":

I simply can't get a good night's sleep in my rollers. I use the "mammoth" size (3″ in diameter) as prescribed in your recent feature "This Was a Real Nice Fundo," and they circle my head completely. When I lay my head down, therefore, it rests on a considerable amount of wire, which is very uneven not to say noisy. Sometimes I can fall asleep sitting up, but only for a few hours. I need nine hours a night. I have lost 30 lbs., my secretarial work is falling off, and I am grumpy and irritable. I'VE GOT TO GET SOME SLEEP! Help me!

SANDRA W.,
Council Bluffs, Iowa

DEAR SANDRA:

Have you tried to sleep standing up? Many girls have found it the perfect answer to the very problem that you describe. If you can't master this little trick, you will just have to remove your rollers at night. You can of course continue to wear them as usual to the office, on dates, at dances, to the beach in summer, to the theater, when entertaining at home, etc., etc. Take them off last thing at night and put them back on first thing in the morning.

*

DEAR "HAIRCURL":

My husband says I've got to "do something" about my hair or he will "leave me." I am twenty-nine and have never let my hair be cut or thinned. When I was married it only came to my waist. Now it falls to the floor (several inches actually drag on the floor) and my husband often trips over it. He says there must be some way to put up hair of this length but my beautician says there isn't. (I think my beautician hates me.) What shall I tell my beautician? What shall I tell my husband?

ANXIOUS,
New Canaan, Conn.

DEAR ANXIOUS:

Of course your husband is right. That hair of yours sounds like a real mess. If you insist on keeping it, the possibilities of a successful "do" are limited. Last year we recommended a beehive upsweep for a lady in Walla-Walla with ankle-length hair. One night while she was asleep a swarm of bees nested in it. She found this impractical and was obliged to dismantle it. Your best bet is the "Topknot Stackup," featured in our July issue, pp. 46 thru 110 with vertical foldout diagram. As you will see, the hair is simply drawn up from the floor, looped twice around the neck clockwise, and tied in a half-hitch that rests squarely on the head. Building on this flat base, your stylist then plaits the strands together, in the manner of weaving a basket, tapering the hairdo gradually as he climbs higher on his ladder, securing it firmly at the top with Scotch tape. Of course this updo cannot be used if your house has low ceilings. Too, it must never be worn if conditions are the least bit windy. Incidentally, you should allow three and a half hours at your beautician's.

*

DEAR "HAIRCURL":

I have always been careful to conceal my curlers under a scarf or babushka, as my steady says he personally thinks that curlers don't "add anything" to a girl's looks. Last summer I bought an unusually big babushka ($3\frac{1}{2}'$ x $2\frac{1}{2}'$) to cover all the curlers required for your "Orbit Out-swirl"—by the way, I think it was thrilling how you dedicated it to the U.S. Space Program—so I assumed I had a scarf to meet any new style that might come up.

Well, I didn't anticipate the "Down-in-Front Roll" featured in your August issue, which you say is going to be all "the rage" this year. As you know, the curlers for this "do" descend in layers down the forehead, and the bottom row is level with the eyelids. This means that the curlers come within $\frac{1}{2}$ inch of obstructing the vision. When I add a scarf, since there is no way to keep it from drooping slightly, it covers my eyes completely.

I have tried to "live with" this arrangement for more than a week, but I find that it interferes with my school-work, and I also feel that my steady is no longer as interested in me. What hope is there for an old-fashioned girl who is only trying to look "decent"?

GROPING,
Seattle

DEAR GROPING:

We have wonderful news for you. Mr. Hud of Beverly Hills has just announced a dramatic breakthrough in this very problem of curler concealment, which has baffled science for so long. He has invented a large bag made of loosely woven vinyl which fits completely over a woman's head, thereby covering every possible type of curler arrangement. The bag has two openings for the eyes, a vent at the mouth for breathing, and, best of all, it comes in thirty-one exciting decorator colors.

Technically the problem was to give the bag enough body so that it would stand free from the "do" and not press against the curlers and clips, yet remain pliable enough to hug the contours of the face. Otherwise it would be too big to be manageable, for at its widest point— slightly above the temples—it adds an estimated three feet to the circumference of the head. The bag recently went into mass production, and Mr. Hud predicts that 87 percent of American women will be wearing bags over their heads by Summer. Thrilling, isn't it?

4. There Are Smiles . . .

ONE EVENT THAT TAKES ME BY SURPRISE every year is the announcement of a new Miss Rheingold. In her picture she looks so much like the old Miss Rheingold—in fact, like all the old Miss Rheingolds—that I can't believe it is not the same girl.

And this is only one of many places where I see her. She is the stewardess in every American airliner, smiling away my fears. She is the girl in every television commercial, smiling away my cramps as she tells me of the pill that consumes thirty-eight times its weight in stomach acids. She is the TV weather girl, smiling that low-pressure area away from my door and assuring me that tomorrow will be fair and warmer. Her name is Miss Legion. She is the all-purpose face of modern America. It is not a face to launch a thousand ships, or even one. It is a face to beach a thousand ships and lull the sailors into a sleep of beautiful dreams.

If there are smiles that make us happy, as the old song claims, there are smiles that make us sick, as the old song doesn't claim, and this smile is one of them. For it grins equally at good things (beer) and bad things (oven grease), serious things (a fire in engine 3) and trivial things (an electric toothbrush), and, in short, all things except funny things, which it wouldn't know if it met one on the street.

Nothing so symbolizes the aggressive blandness of the times as this girl who is all smile and no substance. Don't give anything a second thought, she seems to be saying, or even a first thought. Just sing along with little Mary Sunshine and all the clouds will roll away. She does not, however, symbolize the real American woman. More than ever, the real American woman is a thinking creature. There is far more substance than smile in her concern for the world in which she lives today and in which her children will grow up tomorrow. She gives serious attention to the many different roles that she balances so adroitly from morning to night, and she knows that on the whole they are no laughing matter. The smiling girls don't realize this; they really think that they represent their sex. Obviously it is time for a new symbol—the American woman is taking a bum rap.

Several years ago I thought there was some hope when one of the five finalists in the Rheingold derby was a Miss Garcia. Her four competitors, needless to say, looked identical—this almost seems to be a rule of the contest— but Garcia was something new. For one thing, she looked alive. Her face also had a discernible bone structure, and this set her apart from her rivals, too. For the all-purpose face doesn't have any real features. It is supposed to be round and soft, a powdery ball untouched by life's animating winds, unstamped by experience or ideas.

I knew, of course, that Garcia didn't have a chance, though I dropped into many a tavern during the campaign to vote for her, and, as it turned out, she didn't. Miss Prototype won again and smiled at us for another twelve months out of ski suits, bathing suits, bowling suits and all the other required costumes of happy America, after which another contest was held and she succeeded herself once more.

To some extent, inevitably, Miss Garcia lost because her name was Garcia and she broke the standard North American pattern—still a form of heresy. She was a pioneer, and in years to come, whenever beer drinkers gather to recall the old Rheingold wars, her name will be mentioned with the kind of respect that is accorded our early suffragettes. But her real penalty was that her face was different and interesting. The same handicap would have defeated, say, Sophia Loren if she had come unknown, from another culture, into the finals against four of the smiling no-faces that American industry keeps serving us in its fusillade of vapid cheer.

Surely it is no accident that the airlines hire Miss Prototype to soothe us as we lurch through the stratosphere with intimations of mortality. She doesn't know a turbo prop from a turbot sauté, and we know that she doesn't, but when she appears wreathed in smiles to say that we shouldn't worry about the smoke billowing out of the left wing because the fully automatic smoke-detection-control adjudicator will fix it in a jiffy, we believe her, for is she not the same girl who jollies us through all of life's vexations from sticky dentures to tarry resins?

Not long ago one of the major airlines ran a group picture of its stewardesses in an advertisement, and the effect was positively eerie, for among the hundred rapturous girls there was less genetical variation than Mendel would have thought possible. Some had dark hair and some had blond hair, but otherwise they were pressed out of the same mold. Perhaps there is such a mold, hidden in a cave under the Rockies, unknown even to the F.B.I. and the Better Business Bureau, that has been turning out this repeating model for years.

If so, it is connected to the outside world by a tunnel going both East and West. The East tunnel has an exit in Atlantic City, where fifty identical girls emerge once a year to compete in the Miss America contest, but its real function is to deliver the no-faces to the advertising agencies in midtown Manhattan. Dozens of these girls come up from underground every morning, and before the day is out they are impressed into magazine ads and videotape for the entire nation to see.

Television is, of course, their broadest land of opportunity. For it is not only in the commercials—that beatific realm where girdles never pinch and every nasal sinus is decongested—that their smiling faces are in demand. Equal time is given to them in the editorial programming, so that it is often hard to tell where one category ends and the other begins.

A commercial for detergents can blend into a home-economics show with no change of mood, for in both sequences the girls are having such a good time. It is as much fun to put Timmy's overalls into the sudsy washer as to bake a cake for Daddy's dinner. Of course *nobody* has as much fun as Bess Myerson in the Ajax Stain Center. I have the feeling that Miss Myerson lives in the Stain

Center—a large room full of sinks in various stages of smudge and smudge-removal—and that she lives there by choice. She shows us around it as ecstatically as if she were the curator of Winterthur, her Miss America smile still intact, though her year on the throne expired some time ago. Only the soap-opera heroines, of all the girls on TV, are allowed to don the mask of tragedy, for sorrow is the material that they are expected to purvey. In their periodic brush with adversity they come closer to catching the truth, ironically, than most of the ladies who dominate the television channels.

Even the weather girls keep smiling, whether the skies that they foretell are blue or gray. No hint of tomorrow's hurricane will be divined in their joyous faces. Watch the pleasure with which they roll out the phrase, "Small-craft warnings are up." They know that none of us are in small craft, and that anyone who *is* in a small craft isn't watching television, so they have nothing to lose by telling us. In fact, they have everything to gain. Because most of us are in bed, or at least snug in our homes, we feel all the better for being there and quite proud of ourselves for not being out in a small craft on such a night as this.

Like the airline stewardesses, the weather girls seem to know nothing of the technical mysteries that they explain with such delphic wisdom, but they plunge ahead undaunted, pointing frequently—and with great pleasure—at that occult web of circles and arrows, the weather map. Actually we don't know what the circles and arrows mean any more than the girl does, but we gaze at them enchanted.

The weather map could almost be the heraldic crest of modern America. It is an emblem shown to us by a smiling girl every night before we go to sleep. We don't have to study it because we don't understand it in the first place, and we couldn't do anything about it if we *did* understand it, and yet it reassures us that everyone is pulling hard for a beautiful tomorrow. Knowing this, we drop off more quickly than if we took a sleeping pill. If the next day dawns rainy, we don't hold it against Miss Weather. She did her best, and tomorrow *really* will be better.

As for the tunnel that goes westward from the girl-press under the Rockies, it leads to Hollywood, as anyone will testify who buys a fan magazine and tries to tell one starlet from another. In recent years this genus has been expanded to include "singing stars" as well as movie stars, and it would be reasonable to expect the vocalists to bring some variety to the breed. At least that's what it would be reasonable to expect.

But this is no place for a man of reason to go exploring. Although the captions say that Molly Bee and Sandra Dee are two different girls, that Connie Stevens is not Connie Francis or Ann Francis, that Kathy Nolan is distinct from Kathy Crosby, that Tuesday Weld isn't Wednesday's child and every other child, that Gale Storm isn't Mitzie Gaynor and that all of them are really not Debbie Reynolds, the evidence supporting the captions is not strong.

After all, this girl (whoever she is) is always posed with the same boy. He also goes under many different names—a few of them are Fabian, Frankie Avalon, Tommy Sands, Ricky Nelson, Mark Damon, Bobby Darin, James Darren and John Gavin—but who does he think he's fooling? Not me. It's amazing, though, how many people he *is* fooling. Thousands of teen-age girls really believe that these are different boys and call them by their various aliases.

Unlike the sunny American girl-face, this boy-face runs no risk of killing us with kindness. Generally sullen, but sometimes merely petulant, it probably represents a sub-conscious effort to stem the female tide of empty smiles that has long rolled out of Hollywood and dashed against the American heartland. It is a tide that has always carried its fair share of grinning lasses—ah, there, Virginia Mayo—but never as many as now.

The nation should be grateful to Elizabeth Taylor for muddying the image. Not only is Miss Taylor very beautiful. She also feels no obligation to charm us—she knows instinctively that her message is getting across. She doesn't bubble; she smolders, and she looks as if she wouldn't hesitate to break a man in two if he displeased her. Now that's a face.

But Liz recently turned thirty. She has crossed over into that bourne where yesterday's screen sirens, like Lana Turner, are now playing mothers of teen-age children—passionate mothers, to be sure, in whom the fires of youth are by no means banked, but mothers nonetheless. It will be some time before Elizabeth Taylor agrees to play a mother in the movies—I think we can all count on that—but the fact remains that the generations are changing and no heir is in sight. Are we really to spend the next decade being smiled at by the likes of Molly Bee and Sandra Dee? The times cry out for new tigresses who will keep us on our mettle. If the nation is really serious about physical fitness, that's the place to start.

Miss No-Face is not just a visual phenomenon. There is a voice to match, as every airline passenger knows who has been told to fasten his seat belt during the forthcoming turbulence which won't hurt a bit. It is a voice so coated with sugar that the words lose their individual shape and meaning. They become mere musical tones, rising and falling ever so gently, like the music that is fed to imminent mothers in the labor rooms of certain hospitals to keep them in a contented daze.

It is the voice of the secretary apologizing to a telephone caller because her boss is "engaged" (even if he isn't), or of the girl who has recorded such a message to be played to anyone who calls after the help has gone home. This use of recordings is now so prevalent that a man often doesn't know if he is talking on the phone with a real girl or an artificial one. Usually the recorded voice has an extra degree of stilted sweetness that gives it away, but there can be exceptions, as I found one night not long ago.

The phone rang at home and a girl identified herself as Miss Blank from one of the big dance studios. She congratulated me on my good luck in having my telephone number selected and went on to describe a series of dance lessons, at ludicrously low rates, which I had thereby won. It was a recording if I ever heard one. The voice trilled on with the precision of a machine. Sunlight dropped with special emphasis on just the right word here, the right syllable there, and I could almost reconstruct the recording session at which she had carefully rehearsed these effects and then committed them to wax.

At last her recital came to a pause and, just for fun, I said, "Excuse me, Miss Blank, but are you alive?"

There was no answer. Then, after a moment, the voice said in perfectly modulated tones, "What do you mean?"

"Are you alive," I asked, "or are you recorded?"

This was followed by a very long pause. Finally she said, "Oh, I'm alive." But her voice lacked conviction. She didn't sound as if she meant it, and I'm still not sure she did.

It is not only the tone of the smiling voice that makes it such a good tranquillizer. The voice is also harnessed to a special syntax that has sedative powers of its own. This syntax is dased on the "dangling noun" (the noun that has no article or modifier) and the "dangling verb" (the verb that has no subject), both of which are favorites of the girls who give TV commercials.

The dangling noun was imported from the world of the nurse or dental hygienist who says, "Doctor will see you now." She never says "the doctor" or "Doctor Jones." Doctor is not an individual; he is a larger force, like God, who is all-present and all-healing. On television this usage is frequently given to Baby. He is never "your baby"; he is Everybaby, universal man in diapers, and what's good for him is good for America (and good for General Motors, too).

"Won't hurt Baby's stomach," a smiling girl on TV will say, dangling verb and noun in quick succession.

Who won't hurt Baby's stomach? Does the smiling girl mean that *she* won't hurt Baby's stomach? Probably not. She merely wants to leave the impression—in one rapid burst—that *nobody* is going to hurt Baby's stomach. Stomach-wise, babies are O.K. Baby-wise, stomachs are O.K. The effect is upbeat and yet vague, and that's the beauty of the dangling verb. Like the weather map, it isn't meant to be understood except in the most general way, and neither is the dangling noun.

When the two are used in conjunction, they are hypnotic beyond all resisting, for they take the sharp edges off every sentence. As these sentences are then delivered by smiling girls whose face and voice also have no sharp edges, the listener becomes drowsy with euphoria. It does no good for him to grip his chair and try to hold on to the world around him. The bobbed sentences lilt their promise of health, happiness and instant relief, and reality soon slips away as in in a puff of opium.

"Rubs out dirt . . . sweeps clean too . . . Doctor knows

... acts fast ... coddles Baby ... gives comb-control ... builds Junior's body six ways ... saves Mom ... counteracts the acetylsalicylic acid in ordinary aspirin ... likes Dad ... deep-cleanses sink ... gives Sister underarm protection ... bleaches extra-white ... Doctor says ... contains GL-70 ... contains Doctor ... counteracts Junior ... bleaches Mom ... sweeps Baby extra-clean ... rubs out Dad too ..."

Lulls TV viewer. Falls asleep twice as fast. Sees vision of new America. Four Miss Rheingolds carved in Mount Rushmore. TV weather girl on five-cent stamp. Airline hostesses on penny, nickel, dime, quarter. Bess Myerson and Ajax Stain Center on dollar bill. All look alike six ways. Eliminates work of telling them apart. Counteracts the vitality found in ordinary countries. Sound alike too. Doctor knows. Voices contain deep-acting syrup. Won't hurt anybody. Baby loves their creamy goodness. They're smilier! Stomach tells you so.

5. Saltpeter and the Wolf

teen-age nephew, I soon ran out of topics that bridged his generation and mine, and a painful silence settled over us both. Suddenly I thought of a subject that I knew we would be sure to have in common.

"At your school," I asked, "where do they put the saltpeter?"

He brightened at the question. "It's usually in the mashed potatoes. Where did they put it at your school?"

"Our headmaster got up in the morning and put it in the cream-of-wheat," I said, "but in the army we thought

34

it was in the chipped beef. Tell me: how often do you get it?"

"Once or twice a week," he replied, "and also on special occasions. I mean, the headmaster always puts saltpeter in the food before dances."

"How do you know you're getting it?"

"You can *taste* the stuff," he said.

As we talked on, I was delighted to find that this ancient belief survives as strongly as ever in the nation's youth. For if there is one thing that gives continuity to the galloping generations of American schoolboys, schoolgirls, campers and servicemen, it is the certainty that saltpeter is being slipped into their meals to reduce their sexual urges. In theory this keeps their mind on their work instead of on that other subject, where it is so much more likely to be.

The belief is so old and tantalizing that I decided to track it—if possible—to its source. I began by making a survey of my middle-aged friends, and it turned out to be a surefire topic. All I had to do was drop the word "saltpeter" into a conversation and I might as well have dropped a bomb. People stopped talking about whatever dull topic they were talking about and plunged with relish into this one, their faces alight with a curiosity that time has never quenched. For an aura of mystery continues to surround the saltpeter story. Everybody knows everything about it, and yet—this is the spooky part—nobody knows anything.

Nobody, for instance, has ever witnessed the act of saltpetering the food, though legions of students have kept strict watch during their tour of duty as kitchen help. It is simply assumed that the cook keeps his saltpeter in an unmarked box and that he sprinkles it into the meals with a motion too fast for the human eye, or too casual to arouse suspicion. Nobody seems to know what saltpeter looks like.

Nobody even knows whether it has any effect on the sex glands.

Yet the dread potion still casts fear over the long years of adolescence and early maturity. So closely is it threaded into the American folklore that it even figures in our jokes. Only the other day I heard of a boy entering the army who was worried about his threatened maleness, so he asked his father if the food was saltpetered in *his* army days in World War I.

"Of course," said the father,

"Did it work?" asked the boy.

"You know," the father replied, "it's just beginning to work."

Whether it works is a question, as I found in my survey, that evokes answers of every shade from a resentful "Yes" to a defiant "No." But on one point there is total agreement, and this is the belief that saltpeter is white and that it goes into white or whitish foods. How this hunch arose is not hard to guess, for in the school and camp diet no color comes out of the kitchen with such stunning regularity as no color at all. One might expect—and certainly every parent does expect—the meals to cover nature's spectrum, from red meat to yellow corn to green beans. But it is white that dominates the table, starting with dawn's early farina, continuing with midday's mashed potatoes and ending with supper's flabby puddings.

White sauces are particularly suspicious. Surely it is no accident that chipped beef is such a staple of institutional cooking. Here is a meat that literally swims in a viscous sea—one so devoid of taste and color that it can't contain anything good and therefore must contain saltpeter. Possibly it was even invented for this very purpose, long ago, by a school cook stuck with a medico-culinary problem.

But there are half a dozen other traditional villains. "At our school," one matron in her thirties told me, "I just *know* it was in the fish-eyes." She was referring, of course, to tapioca. The very fact that it bears this generic name is proof of its unpopularity, and this in turn makes it an ideal host for saltpeter, for on the whole saltpeter is identified with foods that nobody likes.

"Our headmaster always put it in the damn cream-of-wheat," a graying alumnus of an Eastern school said, "and that's where my boy says it is at his camp, too. We both hate the stuff."

Another big faction says that it goes into the fish—and with good reason. In the entire realm of cookery there is no substance whiter or drearier than a boarding-school sole or scrod. But this theory has one big flaw—many people don't like fish. They leave it on their plate, or merely pick at it, and so miss their allotted dose of saltpeter.

This is a risk that a wise headmaster would not take. He would more probably go to the other extreme and fix the vanilla ice cream. Many adults believe that this is where they got their saltpeter, and they are still angry about it. "Why do you think the headmaster gave us vanilla ice cream so often?" they asked me, flaring with remembered wrath. They have a point—it makes more sense to lace the coveted ice cream than the hated fish or fish-eyes. The only crueler possibility is that the saltpeter goes into milk, so wholesome and plentiful as to be irresistible to a cook. Holders of this opinion always use the word "foamy" when they recall the pitchers of milk at their school or camp.

But one theory far outnumbers the rest, and that of course is the one that points the finger at mashed potatoes. In part this theory is based on the sheer repetition of mashed potatoes in the school diet. But mainly it is because mashed potatoes have a lumpy quality that the tongue encounters nowhere else. Within their soft white mass dwells a colony of hard little mounds, which could only be induced by some alien element. What more likely element than KNO_3, as saltpeter is known to chemistry?

Confirmed in my own belief that saltpeter goes into white foods, I next wanted to learn how often it is administered. The question is a crucial one, obviously, for anybody who knows the answer can arrange his eating habits accordingly. Most people feel that they got saltpeter once a week, but some feel that they were given a far heavier dose.

"We got it four or five times a week," one man told me. "Our headmaster was a very nervous type."

"Our headmaster," said another, "got up every morning and shook it into the breakfast." Quite a few people, in fact, made this statement and were absolutely sure of it. It was simply the first item on the headmaster's daily schedule.

The dose was also increased (there is almost unanimous agreement here) at times of approaching contact with the opposite sex. "Our food was always saltier near the end of the term," I was told. This was to keep the boys and girls from straying into trouble during vacation and thereby sullying the school's good name. Any boy with hopes of conquest took care not to eat anything white during the pre-holiday week—a tactic which, needless to say, brought him close to starvation. Of all the strands in the saltpeter saga, this is one of the most sinister, for it would enable a headmaster to rule his wards even when they have passed beyond his jurisdiction—when they are, so to speak, operating on their own time. He also cracked down, evidently, just before school dances. "Boy, the Old Man really salted the food then!" many people said.

Nor does the Old Man rule only the boarding-school and summer-camp years. In the later army and navy years he is still on the job, issuing instructions to his lackeys in the mess hall. "I remember pouring saltpeter into the soldiers' meals at an army hospital," a World War I nurse told me, "especially before they went on leave. Those were my orders." And a World War II veteran recalls that his company cook showed him a weekly table of saltpeter doses, which varied with the different army recipes. I never saw such a chart in my own army days, but I did feel that my commanding officers would go to any length to repress me, for they never tired of giving us punitive lectures on "sex hygiene" and grisly films on venereal disease.

Up to this point my survey merely uncovered theories. But I was after facts, if any facts there were in this misty realm of legend and hearsay. I went first to the New York Public Library, which has 127 cards on "saltpeter." Not one, however, dealt with its biological effect or with its use in schools, camps, military institutions, prisons or any other monastic society. In fact, the majority dealt with its use as a fertilizer and as an explosive. I learned, for example, that saltpeter makes a wonderful incendiary bomb. Clearly I was on the wrong track here, to say the least. I had to get nearer the source, so I wrote to two friends who are headmasters of boys' boarding schools and asked them pointblank: "Do you or don't you?"

"I checked with our infirmarian," the first one wrote back, "and she said that when she was in nursing school she heard the same rumor; with a member of our faculty who was an officer in the navy, and he said that the sailors on board ship in the last war were certain that saltpeter was served, but that so far as he could ever ascertain there was nothing to it, and lastly with our school doctor, who again had heard the rumor but had never encountered the application of saltpeter to meals. So I'm forced to conclude that this is just one of those legends that have been passed down through all institutions over the years."

The second headmaster was quite indignant. "I've been in the teaching business a long time," he replied, "and I've been in charge of school kitchens and known the cooks, and it's all a myth. I've been headmaster here for twenty-one years, and frankly I spend as much time with the steward and dietitian as with anyone else in the hope of having the food good, attractive and tasty. I have never heard of any saltpeter being put in our food. As a matter of fact, it's ridiculous to even think about it. So if you want to really know the truth as far as this headmaster is concerned, he has never seen any saltpeter put in the food, he knows nothing of any saltpeter ever having been put in any food, and it is a glorification of the unimportant. At least, if the cooks did it, it was done in a most secret fashion and I never heard about it."

Strong evidence, I had to admit—but not conclusive. Did not both headmasters hedge slightly? You bet your chipped beef they did. I needed something more solid, so I went next to our family doctor.

"It's curious," he said, "but medicine has hardly any use nowadays for potassium nitrate, or saltpeter. There was a time when it was inhaled—or put in cigars—to relieve bronchial spasms. Today we only use it, and not too often, in the treatment of kidney diseases, where we want the potassium. We never want the nitrate, which is actually harmful. In fact, saltpeter is a powerful poison if a person gets too much of it."

"But," I asked, "what about this matter of what it does to—I mean when I was in school we all knew that the headmaster put it—"

"I must say," he broke in, "that I've heard about that all my life, but there's just no medical evidence to support it." He took down two huge books and consulted them. "These are the two old standards of pharmacology—Goodman & Gilman and Edmonds & Gunn—and they don't indicate any such use of potassium nitrate."

"You mean there really isn't—"

"What's more," he said, "potassium nitrate tastes very salty and is extremely hard to disguise, even in a small dose. The therapeutic dose of potassium nitrate as a diuretic in kidney ailments is a half-gram. You put a half-gram of saltpeter in anything and it will be detected. Try it. Stop at the druggist and get a pinch of saltpeter and put it in your coffee, and you'll see for yourself that it's only a myth."

So that was it. I was at the end of the trail. It was only a myth. MYTH! The word suddenly set off a carillon in my head. Any boob knows that myths don't just come from nowhere. They come from somewhere—from some dim land called "race memory," from some cranny of the mind whose messages we receive but indirectly. I hurried over to a psychoanalyst and put my problem to him.

"Oh, that's a very old and interesting legend," he said. "Of course psychiatry has a sound explanation for it. You'll find the basic hypothesis postulated in Freud's 'Totem and Taboo.'"

"Couldn't you just postulate it for me in your own words?" I asked.

"Well, it's quite simple, really. You see, this concept that something is being done to curb sexual impulses must spring from the unconsciousness of the individual, or, in the case of a school, from the collective unconsciousness of all the students. They have to repress the sexual impulse because our society imposes so many taboos, and yet adolescence is a time when these impulses become strong and even chaotic, and this leads to terrible guilt feelings."

"What causes the guilt?"

"A great deal of guilt accompanies masturbatory activities," he said. "For one thing, the fantasies accompanying these activities often center on the young masters' wives. The saltpeter myth is an intra-psychic reaction that the student develops to handle his chaotic thoughts at this age. It's somewhat like a paranoid reaction—though not as strong—because it takes the form of guilt and suspicion. The boy thinks 'They're after me,' or 'The headmaster's going to punish me.' "

"How is this tied in with Freud's theory?" I asked.

"Well, you know Freud felt that all men were constitutionally afraid of their fathers. He theorized that in the first society on earth the sons ultimately slew their fathers and took over the leadership of the tribe, including the sexual rights with their own mothers. In this 'primal parricide,' as Freud called it—and, incidentally, you'll find the tale confirmed in the mythology of many races—the sons incurred overwhelming guilt about the return of the father's spirit and the awful punishment that he would inflict. This punishment would naturally be castration."

"Naturally," I said.

"Now you can see how the saltpeter myth would grow out of all this," the analyst went on. "Saltpeter would temporarily castrate. In the mind of schoolboys or soldiers or sailors it would be the logical step for a headmaster or commanding officer to take as a reprisal for their guilty sexual thoughts. This is why the word goes out, when a ship is approaching port or when a school is about to have a dance, that saltpeter is being put into the food."

"Then it's a group reaction more than an individual reaction?" I asked.

"In general, yes. When a boy goes off to boarding school or camp, he is heavily exposed for the first time to erotic talk about girls. The fact that everyone talks about the subject gives it a collective sanction. And by the same token, the saltpeter is directed by the headmaster at the collective group—at all the young members of the tribe who are becoming aroused by this ritual dance."

"Many of the young members really seem to believe," I said, "that the headmaster goes to the kitchen first thing every morning to pour the saltpeter. How do you explain that?"

"It's all part of the same delusion," he said. "I had a headmaster who lent himself to that kind of omnipotence. He got up early each day and walked over the entire school grounds with an enormous great dane. Any boy seeing him would think of him as the all-seeing, all-knowing chief of the tribe. But he also had your best interests at heart, and that was part of the conflict. If you were being a good boy he was being a good headmaster, and if not you would suspect him of terrible retribution.

"Saltpeter is the perfect punishment, of course, because it's so subtle. You have to eat, so nobody can escape the chief's revenge. You are helpless and choiceless, and it's only what you deserve for the crime that you might even be thinking about girls this way."

I staggered out of the analyst's opaque world into the clear reality of New York City, visions of my own headmaster swirling in my mind. I saw his kindly figure carved into a totem pole with a vial of saltpeter in one hand and a lollipop in the other, and I realized that I had always thought of him, and not of the cook, as the author of our school's saltpeter policy. The cook might have done the actual deed, but he was only an agent for "The Head."

I also concluded that, since the legend is founded in

guilt, it is probably limited to northern countries with repressive and puritanical codes. I doubt if permissive cultures in the Pacific or lusty Latin cultures in the Mediterranean would give house room to such a fearsome myth, and I await the definitive atlas that will indicate—in white —where the world's saltpeter belts lie.

Only one question remained. How, of all the chemical substances that the earth has yielded, did the legend focus on saltpeter? Here again the scholars have been remiss, and the usual dictionaries offer scant help. The sole clue lurks in the unabridged Oxford English Dictionary, which says that one meaning of "saltpeter" derives from the French *la Salpêtrière,* "a hospital for aged and infirm women at Paris, formerly a prison for women." Its English equivalent, says the O.E.D., is "saltpetre house," the first recorded use of which (1767) is: "a woman condemned to be branded and confined to the saltpetre house for nine years."

That the myth came into the Anglo-Saxon world by this route seems a good bet, for prisons have always figured strongly in the legend—if not as strongly as schools, camps and army bases, that is only because fewer people have come out into polite society to tell the tale. But the sexual problems of jail inmates are proverbial, and a rumor could easily have swept some early English "saltpetre house" that the warden was putting a white powder into the food to curb the prisoners' appetites.

As for the origin of *la Salpêtrière,* I have a hunch that Saltpeter and Saint Peter are subtly interwined—or were several centuries ago—but I'll leave that to other researchers. My own investigation ended with a stop at the druggist, who measured out a half-gram of saltpeter and gave it to me. I took it home with trembling hands—here at last I was face to face with the enemy. The powder was, not at all to my surprise, white. The crystals were larger than ordinary salt, but they could easily be ground up into, say, mashed potatoes or fish-eyes or vanilla ice cream. I dumped the little grains into a cup of coffee and they dissolved instantly. No man would know, at least by looking, that the coffee had been treated.

Shakily I lifted the cup and took a sip. It tasted terrible. I started to take another swallow, but some invisible force —some primal instinct that came from I know not where —pushed my hand back to the table. I took the cup out to the kitchen and poured the coffee down the drain. A man can't be too careful.

6. Broadway Bound

(Three dramatists describe their incoming plays in the Sunday drama section of the "New York Times")

By PAUL PLOVER
Author of "Say Dad, Is That Thomas Wolfe at My Door?," opening Wednesday at the Belasco

AS A DRAMATIST WHO IS ABOUT TO THROW his hat in the Broadway ring, I was deeply interested in the two articles by playwrights which recently ran in your respected columns, namely the piece by Dana Dotard, "grand old man of the American realistic theater," charging that Edward Alboo's "theater of the absurd" was "an absurdly absurd travesty of true drama," and Mr. Alboo's reply that it was absurd for Mr. Dotard to say that the theater of the absurd was absurdly absurd. I'm sure your readers followed this penetrating exchange with the same keen delight as I.

46

I have a particular interest in the debate because my own position as a playwright happens to fall between these two extremes. Curiously, in fact, one newspaper in Dallas, where my play was given a luminous performance by Workshop 1970 last summer in connection with the Writers' Conference and Arts Festival of Lower Magruder County, referred to me as "an absurd realist." As you undoubtedly know, Workshop 1970 is the experimental group that produces plays without sets, costumes, props or actors. The dialogue is recorded on tape and piped up through grates in the auditorium floor. Thus the audience enjoys the thrill of a shared dramatic experience without the usual distractions to the eye, and the playwright is freed once and for all from his ancient enemy, the proscenium arch.

Actually, as I say, my own position is not that "far out." While I agree with Mr. Alboo that we must "overthrow the false gods of orthodox dramaturgy," since, as he puts it so brilliantly, "meaning isn't meaningful until it becomes meaningless," I also agree with Mr. Dotard that "they'll never get rid of the telephone, the butler/maid, and that rich lexicon of phrases on which Western drama has flowered, viz., 'Where are you going, Millie?,' 'Mr. Parker will be back soon' and the like, which are the working tools by which playwrights since ancient Greece have told their spectators what is happening."

"Does Mr. Alboo want to throw all this away?" Mr. Dotard asks in conclusion, and that is the central question to which I addressed myself in writing "Say Dad, Is That Thomas Wolfe at My Door?," which opens Wednesday at the Belasco. Whether I have found a viable answer only the critics will tell me. (Of course critics can be wrong— one remembers Sven Hjølfqvist's statement that "Hedda Gabler" was "a hopeless mishmash"—but there is no blinking the fact that, given the economic structure of the

commercial Broadway theater today, they do wield
tremendous power.) What I have attempted to do, at any
rate, is to achieve a fusion of the two styles, alternating the
absurd and the naturalistic to achieve a wholly new genre.

I realize that there are dangers inherent in such a
flirtation with the untried, but if one is to grow one must
be willing to take risks. In that connection I want to pay
tribute right here to my producer, Dwight McDougal.
Dwight is often accused of being an arid intellectual, but
when he talks of the experimental theater he breathes fire.
He has spared no effort to make this production a living
testimony that the avant-garde has a soul, and his idea
of bringing Don Cucamonga out of retirement to play the
hippopotamus that turns into a twelve-year-old boy was
a stroke of pure genius.

Many people have asked me, "What is your play about?"
They mean well, but, like Mr. Alboo, I am appalled by the
question. It simply does not conduce to an answer. In the
theater of the absurd—or, in my case, the semi-absurd—
a playwright is obviously not trying to "say" anything at
all. The moment, in fact, when he so loses control that
the audience thinks "He's trying to say such-and-such," his
play fails. The spectators must never be permitted to grasp
a point, as it were, directly—that is, by the process of
thought. They must merely apprehend certain vague truths.
Hence it is perfectly proper for friends of the dramatist to
ask, "What vague truths are you trying to intimate?"

When friends put the question to me in this form—
actually nobody has thus far—I can tell them, without
compromising my honor, that "Say Dad, Is That Thomas
Wolfe at My Door?" is not a drama *qua* drama, but rather
an ambiance, which, through the catatonic repetition of
various words, deceptively simple in themselves but
freighted with emotion when used in conjunction with

other word clusters, suggests the ultimate truth about urban life at mid-century, which is, of course, the inability of people to communicate with each other. The fact that the playwright is intentionally non-communicating with his audience is the irony that gives the form its underlying strength.

Now it is my personal belief—call it a crotchet, if you will—that such a play tends to become slightly monotonous if it runs from 7:45 to 11:20 without an intermission, as mine did in its first experimental production two summers ago in Vermont at the Green Mountain Festival of Performing Arts, held in association with the Meat Loaf Poets' Conference, and accordingly I reshaped it into its present unusual form.

The scheme now is as follows: Acts I and III are frankly naturalistic. There are props, sets, costumes, etc., and in the dialogue there is no attempt whatever to mystify the audience. On the contrary, the listener is given many plain guides to the action, as, for example, in the chambermaid's line: "She just went down to the A. & P." The actors speak to each other as in normal conversation, not obliquely; the hippopotamus does not appear, nor do the three old ladies who live in empty refrigerators.

Acts II and IV, by contrast, are the "release." As I have explained to my seminar in Obscurantism 201 at Sarah Lawrence, they are like the systole and diastole of the human heartbeat, or the flow and ebb of the tide, and it is this cyclical law of nature that I have tried to adapt to dramatic purpose. The contrast is instantly noticeable to the theatergoer when the house lights dim for Act II, because the curtain does not rise on the stage where Act I took place. Instead, the actors are discovered to be on an aluminum disc suspended by thin wires approximately twenty feet above the audience's head.

This floating stage is, I feel, the long-sought answer to the quest for a true theater-in-the-round. Its sole disadvantage is that people with seats in Rows F through P, being directly under the disc, can see none of the action, though the timbre of the actors' voices, reverberating off the side walls and then down to those particular seats, has an ethereal quality which more than compensates for the absence of good "sight lines."

You can readily imagine that the audacious platform, so aloof from all fetters of time and place, cries out to the dramatist to strike off the chains of syntax. "Logic, begone!" it seems to say. Then the playwright, like the abstract painter, must splash his colors on in bold rhythms, never pausing to ask what he is doing, lest, heaven help him, he should find out. This is the heady thrill of creation which I am proud to share with Mr. Alboo—and which Mr. Dotard, alas, will never know.

Are you perhaps wondering if I envy Mr. Dotard the $940,000 advance sale already compiled by the musical play that he has written for Mary Martin, "The Sound of Albert Schweitzer"? Don't be absurd.

*

By PETER COOKOUT
*Writer-star of the British topical-satirical
revue, "Come What Mayfair," due Thurs-
day at the Helen Hayes*

One feels a certain diffidence—one almost wants to say fright—when one brings a work like "Come What Mayfair" to Broadway for the first time in one's career. One's feeling is not occasioned by the fact that one is only nineteen. One has, after all, been hailed in one's own country since the age of twelve, when one came down from Oxbridge, as a wit of dazzling precocity. One has tilted one's lance at Whitehall, Downing Street, Westminster Abbey, indeed even at Buckingham Palace, and seen them quaver. One inevitably finds this satisfying.

No; it is rather because one has never been to America before and one knows that the climate is not—indeed cannot hope to be—ready for one's particular kind of intellectual sport. One knows that in America there is no common university culture of the sort which, in one's own country, produces not only the brilliant topical satirist—one is thinking especially of oneself and one's three colleagues in "Come What Mayfair"—but also produces an audience sufficiently educated to appreciate the satire that one does. One cannot help feeling, therefore, that one is bringing jewels into the desert. Nevertheless, when one is the vanguard of topical satire, one has a sacred trust. One must keep going. Otherwise, one cannot call oneself a vanguard, can one?

One has heard it said that topical satire has in fact been introduced to America already: by other Americans. One recalls favourable mention of Mr. Sahl, of Mr. Nichols and Miss May, of the "Premise" cabaret and other ironical dabblers. One cannot question the undoubted sincerity of these efforts by the colonials to emulate a generic English form. Still, one does find these pretensions off-putting. Even though one has never been to America, one knows what it is like. One knows that the spirit of Senator McCarthy still reigns and that the country is ridden with taboos. Patently Mr. Sahl and his fellow "humourists" have not been dealing in satire as it is known in the older cultures, but merely in vaudeville skits of the most superficial nature.

One is, of course, surprised to learn that one's revue is

booked for fifty-three Broadway theater parties in its first two months. One can only assume that American audiences are attending "Come What Mayfair" for reasons of status having no relation to the show's content, this being, unavoidably, a cerebral exercise of the most rarefied intensity.

One wants to be understood for what one is trying to do. One therefore feels that perhaps one oughtn't to have agreed to remain with "Come What Mayfair" for the two years which its engagement now appears certain to run at the Helen Hayes, or to have also accepted, on behalf of oneself and one's three colleagues, a heavy burden of theater, cinema, night club, restaurant, television, wireless, magazine, newspaper and record contracts lasting until 1972. One undertakes these contracts only because one feels a duty to the American people to remain in their midst for a decade and to speak out with authority and a healthy criticism on their way of life. It is the very least that one can do. Besides, one needs the money.

*

By FRED FRAGONARD

*Author of the book and lyrics of "Moby
Dick," the new musical opening Tuesday
at the Broadhurst.*

PHILADELPHIA.—The editor of the Sunday drama section has asked me to write a little piece explaining how we made "Moby Dick" into a musical. I hardly know where to begin, so thickly do the memories and heartaches come flooding back. It has been seven years of solid work, trying to harness the raw power of Herman Melville's masterpiece, to make it come alive as musical theater. Jack Ripon, who composed the haunting score, and I are satisfied that we have done our best, yet we well know that we are not the

final judges. The final judge is that most wonderful, exhilarating, stimulating and, yes, exasperating, creature of
all: The Audience. In other words, You. If "Moby Dick"
pleases you, we've done our job. If not, the fact that *we*
think we have a beautiful show is of no relevance.

I am writing this in my room in the Warwick Hotel.
There's nothing more that I can do now. Last night Bobby
Tremayne, our tremendously gifted young director, said
"Freeze it!" and we all let out a whoop. I've been associated
with a lot of shows since I contributed my first lyric, "Ooh-
ooh, You-oo," to a little something that you older folks
may remember, "Hips 'n' Pips," back in 1938, but I want
to say right now that I've never seen such a wonderful spirit
in any company as in this one. The "kids" have been really
incredible.

I recall one incident involving Sid Sidney, who, by the
way, is a very big talent; in fact, I'll go way out on a limb
and predict that a new stage personality is going to be
born Tuesday night at the Broadhurst. Sid plays Starbuck,
the first mate on the "Pequod," and we had given him a
solo called "Blind Obsession," in which he muses that
Captain Ahab is going mad and will take the ship to its
doom.

Somehow the number never "caught fire," so Jack and I
decided to change the mood, and one night we batted out a
catchy little tune called "Crazy Old Man," which Starbuck
could sing with the entire men's chorus. We gave it to
Sid and the kids on Wednesday morning, and also to
"Sunny" Hornpipe, our choreographer who has created
such a stunning harpoon ballet, and they did it that same
afternoon in the matinee. Unfortunately, that number
never caught fire either, so we took out the whole scene,
but it shows you what I mean about the wonderful spirit
in this company.

But I'm getting off the subject of how "Moby Dick" was

born. I remember clearly it was in 1956, just a few weeks after our musical adaptation of "The House of the Seven Gables" had closed in Wilmington after three days of its pre-Broadway tryout. Naturally Jack and I were disappointed that it had such a short run, and to this day we wonder if it wasn't too "special" for Wilmington and we should have opened cold on Broadway, where a creative artist isn't penalized for being "different." Anyway, we were eager to find a new property—one that told a rousing yarn and still, quite frankly, had "guts."

This may sound pretentious, but I happen to feel that the American musical theater has grown up and is flexing its muscles. It isn't the simple, uncomplicated child it was when I broke into this field. You can't just have a good-looking tenor come out and sing "I love you" to some cute little ingenue. Every musical number, be it a song or a dance or what-have-you, has got to establish character and further the plot. Nowadays you've got to throw away the rule book and keep breaking new ground. At least this is how Jack and I work—you might say it's our basic philosophy—so when our agent said one Sunday afternoon, when we were sitting around my pool in Bucks County, that his daughter had telephoned from Miss Smithers' School and happened to mention that she was writing a theme on "a terribly dramatic book called 'Moby Dick' with the most fascinating hero since Yul Brynner in 'The King and I,'" we both jumped up and said, "That's it!"

Even before we wrote a note the property had a lot of merit, and I don't mean only that it is in the public domain and we didn't have to buy the rights. Take the historical period, for example. The nineteenth century is only the most romantic century there ever was. And the locale. We start in New England, which is austere and quaint, and go to the South Sea Islands, which are lush and voluptuous. That's contrast, or I miss my bet, and when you see Peggy LaRochefoucauld's fabulous sets you'll agree.

And right between those two extremes is The Sea, which I like to think is our other main character. It's savage and elemental, yet placid and beautiful, and we've tried to capture this strange dualism in the nine-minute cantata that ends Act I. The words are sung by Queequeg, the Indian harpooner who has never been to sea before and can't understand why it's calm one day and angry the next, and the men's chorus represents the ocean in its various shifting moods.

Jack's music is so absolutely right I kid him that I get seasick whenever I listen to it, but seriously, when you hear the fabulous bassoon theme that represents the creaking of the ship's hull in a typhoon, you'll agree. Some people told us that it's too "advanced" for Broadway. This may sound pretentious, but I believe Broadway is ready for this score. People also told us that audiences wouldn't "get" the limping meter, symbolizing Ahab's wooden leg when he walks the deck, that we built into his second-act soliloquy:

Oh WHALE ma-LEV-o-LENT and WHITE,
Who LONG a-GO bit OFF my LEG,
Where ARE you WHALE, come OUT and FIGHT,
I'm GON-na TAKE you DOWN a PEG.*

I think audiences will hear that that lyric definitely has a limp.

One more thing and then I'll let you good people get back to your Sunday breakfast. I hear you saying that the "Pequod" never put in at any South Sea Islands. If you want to be technical, that's true. But Jack and I felt that we were entitled to some "artists' license." The "Pequod" doesn't have any women aboard, remember, so we have no feminine interest after the scene early in Act I—it follows the opening ballad, "Call Me Ishmael," that Roddy Blau does so unforgettably—where the womenfolk of New Bedford gather on the wharf and sing the farewell hymn, "Thar She Goes!" (This melody, incidentally, is reprised to a different lyric, "Thar She Blows!," in Act II when a whale is sighted off the Galapagos, which is what I mean by the American musical theater growing up into an integrated whole.)

The New Bedford ladies are all bundled up in long crinoline skirts, naturally, and we felt that the audience would want to look at a different kind of girl after going to sea on the "Pequod" for four years—and so would the crew of the "Pequod." In other words, there is sound motivation for the scene where they put in at Bora-Bora for a load of breadfruit, and when you see the fabulous grass G-strings and bras that Babs O'Toole designed, you'll agree.

I won't spoil the show for you by giving away any more of our secrets. I've told you this much because I wanted to assure you that we have not violated the integrity of Melville's great classic, but have handled it with reverence and even, hopefully, given it a new dimension. If so, I can only say with deep humility that I'm sorry Herman Melville won't be sitting in the Broadhurst Theater on Tuesday night. My mother will, but she never read the book.

7. *A Little Flight Music*

GOOD MORNING, LADIES AND GENTLEMEN. This is Captain Smathers welcoming you aboard your Peerless Airlines DC-80 Jetfloater flight 902 to Los Angeles. Our movie today will be the adult Biblical epic, "The Passionate Legions," in CineMagic x80, starring Charlton Lancaster and Sophia Lollobrigida and featuring Walter Brennan as the Emperor Diocletian. Your air hostess, Miss Smiley, will start the movie as soon as the aircraft is aloft and the "No Smoking" sign is off. We estimate that the picture will run four hours and eleven minutes, with an intermission after the burning of Smyrna, at which time we will land at Omaha for refueling and popcorn. Passengers disembarking at Omaha may ask Miss Smiley for a synopsis of the remainder of the film, or write directly to Epic Pictures, Aviation Division, Hollywood 33. We expect to be cruising at an altitude of 18,000 feet, but the cabin is pressurized starting at three feet, so you should experience no discomfort. Our air speed will be approximately 300 miles per hour and our ground speed will be 200 miles per hour. This discrepancy, caused by the fact that the earth is round and the air is flat, is fully explained in the informative booklet, "You and Your Flight!," which will be found in the pocket directly ahead of you, next to the airsickness bag, which you may want to use during the scene when ten Christian martyrs are mangled by tigers in the arena at Antioch. This scene should begin shortly after we cross the Mississippi River at Moline and will conclude ten minutes after Cedar Rapids. I will be pointing out to you certain interesting sights along the way. Meanwhile, Miss Smiley and the rest of your Jetfloater crew join me in hoping that you enjoy the movie. We'll be taking off in just a minute now, as soon as we get clearance from the tower. There are only twenty-three planes stacked up over the field waiting to land, and right after that we'll be off. By the way, that roaring you hear under the left wing is nothing to worry about. We had a little trouble with the automatic desludgifier a while ago, and that noise is simply the cleaning compound doing its job. Good morning, ladies and gentlemen, this is your air hostess, Miss Smiley. I'm sorry we were so long in getting clearance. You may unfasten your seat belts now and stop observing the "No Smoking" sign. In a minute Miss Mirth and I will serve you cocktails and start the movie projector. If there is anything that you do not understand about the movie, please do not hesitate to ask us. Simply press the button next to the reading light except on seats 9, 17, 24, 36, 48, 59, 71, 86 and 101, which are the emergency escape doors. Kindly do not leave by these doors while the movie is in progress. . . . *Oh, Smartacus, thank God you've come! The Roman columns are marching toward Byblos at this very moment. What*

chance has a poor slave girl like me got against such
Barbarian swine? . . . Never fear, my pretty little Flolita.
Take these two thousand piastres and run to Damascus over
the Baalbek road. Go to a man called Paul in a street called
straight and tell him I will join you there as soon as the
moon comes over Mountolive. Tell him . . . Hello again,
ladies and gentlemen, this is Captain Smathers. If the screen
is a bit wiggly, we're encountering a little weather, but we
should be out of it in another twenty minutes, I hope in
time for the boiling oil scene. That girl, by the way, is
Sophia Lollobrigida. You'll see when the screen is clearer.
. . . Say, you're a tasty little dish of figs, aren't you? What's
a looker like you doing all alone on the road to Damascus?
Notice how easily my fingers press into your pretty white
flesh. . . . Leave me be, you heathen beast! When Smartacus
hears about this, he'll squash you like the foul insect you
are! . . . Aha! I've been trying to trap Smartacus for three
long years. With you as bait he's sure to . . . Ladies and
gentlemen, Federal regulations require that when flying
over land we demonstrate this life preserver, which you will
find under your seat. As you see, it is easy to operate. Simply
pull the red toggle knob downward with a sharp thrust,
like this, and if it fails to open, simply tug the green
counterloop sideways with a revolving motion, like this,
which activates the flare dispatcher, the flashlight, the
whistle and the zipper. One precaution: do not effectuate
these steps while you are still inside the aircraft as that
will markedly hamper your escape. Thank you. . . . But
Paul, how can we warn Smartacus in time? . . . Tut, tut,
my child, you must have faith. Was it not said in Galilee
that the wicked would fall like wheat? Besides, I know a
certain pharmacist in Aleppo who . . . Say, folks, in just a
minute you're going to get a dandy view of Sandusky, Ohio,
out the left window. We don't often see it as clear. Sandusky
is known for its jute mills and crampon factories. You can

just see them now beyond that bend in Route 37A off to the left. . . . *Begging your pardon, Emperor, but why should we worry about a little handful of religious nuts? . . . You're young, my boy. Maybe when you get a little older you'll see that faith can be a mighty potent weapon. . . . All I know, Emperor, is if you'll give me a hundred men and ten lions I'll clean those religiosos out fast. That's what your Uncle Caligula would have done. . . . Hmmm, perhaps it's worth a try. . . .* Ladies and gentlemen, we've just heard that Omaha is closed in. They're having a bit of weather down there. Hurricane Zula got up from Shreveport faster than anyone expected. We're going to put back to Bermuda, but don't worry, we won't interrupt the movie, and if it ends before we get down, we've got another movie aboard, Jerry Waldo's super-adult drama for adults only, "We Were Adulterers!" . . . *But Paul, how did you know the Emperor's lions wouldn't harm us? It was a miracle like how they turned on Diocletian's mercenaries instead. . . . My child, things happen that man in his vanity can never fathom. How can I make you understand? Perhaps if I recall an event that took place long ago beside a date palm in Jerusalem. I was sitting* . . . Ladies and gentlemen, this is Miss Smiley. During this flashback, which isn't very interesting, Miss Mirth and I are going to serve you your Jetfloater dinner, prepared for your eating pleasure in our Jetfloater kitchens in Pocatello Falls, Idaho. Miss Mirth and I regret that we cannot serve you your dinner and keep the movie in focus at the same time, especially during the electrical storm that we are about to pass through. But as soon as your Jetfloater dinner is over we will pick up with the siege of Ephesus, which was filmed with a cast of thousands on location outside Ephesus, Illinois, with the full cooperation of the Illinois government. Meanwhile, please fasten your seat belts again. We *do* hope you are enjoying your movie and your flight.

8. Sex and the Grammar School Girl

FRANKLY, I WAS SHOCKED WHEN THE editor asked me to write an article on "Sex and the Grammar School Girl." When I was a grammar school girl, not too long ago, we were interested mostly in playing jumprope. Yet here was the editor of a famous national magazine saying to me pointblank: "Do you think chastity has a chance in grammar school today?"

"Why," I gasped, "these girls are only six to eleven years old."

"You're behind the times," the editor rebuked me. "Don't you know there has been a sharp turn away from traditional sex morality? 'Old-fashioned' standards are being questioned by the modern girl and found wanting."

"But surely," I protested, "this questioning doesn't begin so young." I am known as a hard-bitten girl reporter who has seen everything, but even I was shocked at what I was hearing, and I guess my face showed it.

"If you don't believe me," the editor persevered, "why don't you go back to your own alma mater and conduct an in-depth survey? Prove out the facts and then write your article."

I agreed, and frankly I guess it was because I wanted to prove the editor wrong. I thought a lot about my assignment as I drove across the country. My destination was Jasper G. Parmelee Elementary School in Wheat Husk, Nebraska, the very heartland of Midwestern conservatism. There, if anywhere, the traditional American values would be intact, and when at last I drove up to the steps of good old Parmelee I was sure of it.

The school looked the same as when I graduated in 1948. In the playground most of the girls were jumping rope and playing jacks. A few were making mud pies and one was holding a teddy bear. Not until I wandered over near the jungle gym did I detect a mood subtly different from the one I had known in my own carefree school days. A dozen girls about eight years old were sitting in a circle on the asphalt, their lollipops almost untouched as they thrashed out a problem. Their faces reflected an inner bewilderment.

One of them, a pretty child I'll call Betsy, was saying: "At first I just let him sharpen my pencils. Then he wanted to carry my books, and I let him do that too. If I hadn't, I was afraid I would lose him."

"It's so hard to know what to believe," chimed in

Sally Lou. "It was easy for our mothers—they had a clearly defined set of 'dos' and 'don'ts.' "

"But now," agreed Terry, cute as a button in her snow-suit, "there's a huge gap between the sexual code that our society professes and the actual behavior that we see among our elders and on the screen."

"It's all part of the throwing off of the shackles of Victorianism," said Gloria, who, at nine, seemed older and wiser than the others. "Censorship laws are breaking down, divorce is commonplace, and there's even a growing tolerance of infidelity among persons who hold high public office." She spun her top angrily across the hopscotch court.

"You're right, Gloria," said bright-eyed little Pam. "Any way you look at it, there's a sexual revolution in America."

"No wonder we're anxious and confused," piped up Patty, fingering a loose tooth. "If only the principal would give us some definite rules. I'd be grateful for a 3:00 P.M. curfew. When Georgie walks me home I'm never sure I can hold out till 4:00. He's not the type of boy who'll take 'no' for an answer. After all, he's ten."

I was startled by the candor of the discussion, which would have been out of the question in my days at Parmelee. I could only conclude that the subject of sex is being confronted far more openly than in previous genera-tions. I asked the girls if they would mind if I took notes for my in-depth survey. I was afraid they might be embar-rassed.

"Mind!" squealed Jeanie, a vivacious little blonde who, I learned, was only seven. "Of course we don't mind! Our generation is eager to confront the subject of sex openly and not bottle it up as previous generations did. We are asking for answers which society may not as yet be prepared to give us."

"Ours is a crisis of identity," elaborated Debbie, a

freckle-faced moppet in jumper and knee socks. "Most of us were brought up to believe that 'nice girls don't.' But here at Parmelee we find that they do. Sex is no longer the private preserve of the intellectual and the Bohemian."

"No doubt about it," Linda joined in, looking up from her copy of "The Cat in the Hat." "The ordinary middle-class average-home sub-teenager is discussing, sifting, experimenting as never before." She was a serious young thing—intense and deeply troubled, I could tell, by the sexual emancipation which, together with the emotional turmoil caused by the war and an increasing acceptance of the Freudian ethic and Existentialist philosophy, coupled with the very real fears of a nuclear holocaust, had cast her adrift from the age-old moorings of strict family and church taboos.

"When you get to grammar school," Gloria explained, tightening her roller skates, "you're subjected to all sorts of peer-group pressures. If a girl is still defending chastity at the age of nine she's regarded as some kind of square."

Yet I had the feeling, looking at Gloria, studying the conflicting emotions that America's sex revolution had thrust on her at such a cruelly early age, that she still believed—desperately wanted to believe—that the "old-fashioned" standards continued to hold validity for girls of her generation. She blew her bubble gum nervously in and out.

"What confuses me," said Terry, the braces on her teeth agleam in the morning sun, "is the apparent disparity between sex which represents the fulfillment of love, on the one hand, and sex as a mere advertising device cynically used by American business to help sell its products."

"For me it has no meaning unless there's love," volunteered Betsy, and when several other girls nodded their agreement I realized that I had stumbled on a cardinal point of the new sex ethic. The grammar school girl is definitely not "loose." If she "plays house" it is only with her steady, and then only when he has given her his Big League Gum collection.

"It's something every girl must decide individually," Jeanie assented, cradling her Barbie doll. "What's right for you may be wrong for me. I know a few of us feel that 'Something within just won't let us go all the way.'"

"That's right," echoed Betsy, "it can only lead to self-hatred and a very real distaste for oneself."

"And yet," Jeanie continued, talking very quietly so as not to wake her Barbie doll, "far be it from me to go around voicing a lot of 'uncool' slogans about virginity and religion. After all, one out of six grammar school girls is already married—some before they even get to long division."

"Not to mention the high drop-out rate which can be traced to many of these same factors," said Sally Lou. "Don't forget our world could be destroyed tomorrow by a nuclear holocaust."

So I was right about that! It *was* on their minds. I felt a sudden stab of anger that my generation had made such a muddle of the world that these kids would inherit, and I hoped they would make a better job of it than we had. Were we to blame, I wondered, for not giving them more rigid tenets of right and wrong in the matter of sex? Or had we been too rigid—and thus driven them to break the bonds of inhibition which have been the American legacy since the days of our Puritan forefathers?

"Tell me," I said, eager to dig out the answer, however painful it might be to the ego of my generation, "do you ever hear any approval from your parents for being a 'nice' girl? Let me put it another way: is there any premium on chastity in grammar school?"

"No!" they chorused emphatically.

"And the tragic part of it is," added Patty, "that we hunger for some indication from our parents that we are right when we discourage intimacy. If they would just say some little thing like 'You're wise to wait until junior high.' "

"Like for instance last week," Betsy blurted out, twisting her braids over and over as she unburdened an experience that had obviously distressed her, "Billy walked me home after school. I let him buy me a Milky Way and a 'Lassie' magazine at the drugstore, so when we got to our porch he felt he was entitled to ask for a lemonade, so I gave him that, but he still wasn't satisfied. We sat there on the glider, and before I could stop him he insisted on having some cookies, and I thought 'I've got to draw the line somewhere,' but I didn't until things had gone almost too far, and I finally sent him away quite sternly, just as my dad was coming home for supper. My dad heard me tell Billy that I was not that kind of girl, and he could have come to me later and said 'I'm glad to see that chastity has a chance in grammar school today,' but he didn't."

"I honestly don't think we should be too hard on our parents," interjected Gloria, and again I was struck by the maturity with which this earnest nine-year-old had puzzled out the moral imperatives of American life at mid-century. "Our elders are as baffled as we are by the perplexing alternatives posed by the permissive temper of the times."

"Nor," put in Liza, "have school administrators or clergymen of every faith been able to hammer out a viable creed for the 'obsexed' culture in which we live. If only . . ."

The rest of her sentence was drowned by the familiar school bell, tolling the end of recess. "Golly," said little Pam, "we better hurry or we'll be late for spelling. You know how mad Miss Naphtha gets." And before I could say goodbye they gathered up their jump ropes and jacks and skipped into the school building, trailing girlish giggles.

How long I sat there after they left I'll never be able to say, but it must have been at least an hour. These young girls had moved me deeply with their agonized quest for moral certitudes in an age of constantly shifting values, and I suddenly knew that I owed it to them to write up my in-depth survey. I had a story for all America to read—and re-read. I thought of Gloria, Sally Lou, little Pam and the others, and silently prayed for the strength to tell their story well. For it really was their story, not mine.

9. *Down to the Sea in Drapes*

OUR TOWN USED TO GET ALONG FINE WITH a plain municipal dock. Now it also has a marina and a boatel—proof that the number of pleasure boats is growing fast and so is the American language.

Every spring, when the seagulls come back from Capistrano and the sun comes back from wherever it has been, the marina and boatel stir with activity. Big motorboats begin to arrive, often in such volume that they are triple-parked, and families on the outer craft have to clamber across the intervening ones to reach land, supermarket and movie house.

The annual invasion makes me wonder what sort of man this seagoing householder is and what impulses take him, however briefly, to sea. Obviously he is not performing a sport, for he runs his boat by machinery—not, as the sailor does, by engaging the wind and water in direct combat. Nor does he seem to seek the water in order to forget the cares of shore. On the contrary, he surrounds himself with the artifacts of modern society. Even when his boat is moving, he sits on the deck in a comfortable chair, drink in hand and awning overhead, reading or playing bridge or listening to the radio, and hardly glancing at the sky above him or the waves below.

Sometimes I try to glimpse the interiors of the motor-boats that are stopping in our marina, and am rewarded with scenes so homey that I might almost be peering into a picture window in Scarsdale. I see curtains on the wall, a dog curled up on the sofa, a TV set on the table and Daddy reading the "Wall Street Journal"—sights not commonly identified with seafaring. Curious to know more about this way of life, I decided to visit the Boat Show when it came to New York.

At first the Boat Show seemed a world in hopeless disharmony. All 450 boats were out of water, the one place where a boat ought not to be. High and dry on the hard Coliseum floor they sat, impotent and pathetic. Some sailboats had their masts cut down to accommodate a low ceiling—misbegotten creatures shorn of their birthright. Over every boat scrambled sales clerks, men in winter overcoats and felt hats, and ladies in furs and high heels.

Amid these alien garments the eye hungered for denim and oilcloth, for torn sweaters and soggy sneakers, and after a while the imagination mercifully supplied them, just as it rigged every sailboat in sail, put waves under every hull and installed a sun-bathing blonde on every deck.

Nothing, however, supplied the tang of salt air or the noises of water. Only the relentless scuffle of shoes filled the hall as men and women trudged from boat to boat, and from booth to booth, to see the latest thing in marine design and gear.

Forgotten was the hostility that divides the boating clan in summer. Then the man of sail scorns the man of motor, this heathen who sullies the afternoon with rude billows and mechanical roars, and the motorboat man views with distaste the hundreds of sails that keep bobbing across his path in meaningless patterns. At the Boat Show they were at least brought under one roof by a common zeal.

Still, each faction was glad to go its own way. The man examining a sailboat, savoring its clean new canvas and shiny brass tackle, didn't covet the power launches near by, where the talk was not of main sheets but bed sheets. Nor did the motorboat customer have anything but pity for the benighted sailors far below him as he relaxed into a deck chair and pictured himself, in yachting cap and blazer, gliding across the water, boatel-bound.

The motorboats, seen from below, looked enormous. Their prows loomed overhead, and it was hard to believe that ordinary citizens, not old Cunard captains, were to buy them. The biggest ones could be seen "by appointment only"—a system designed to separate the interested rich from the inquisitive poor. As the prices ran as high as $86,000, the poor were in something of a majority, and they got their look by climbing up wooden ramps adjacent to the boats and peeking in the windows.

To think of "windows," rather than portholes, was natural, almost obligatory, as I found when I went aboard these luxurious launches (if one "goes aboard" a vessel that is resting on cement). In none of them did I have the feeling that I was on a boat, so cleverly had the naval skeleton been clothed in the silks of interior decoration. Soft pastel rugs covered every floor—gunwale-to-gunwale carpeting, so to speak—and the windows had curtains and screens. All the windows were square or rectangular. The only round one was on a door that divided a living room from a kitchen (i.e., a saloon from a galley), and I noticed it only because a man pointed it out to his wife. "Look, honey," he said, "here's a cute touch."

The furniture varied in detail from one boat to another, but not in mood. Every room had the clean modernistic lines of a Hilton hotel suite. The fabrics on the couches and chairs were in "decorator colors," though one boat had a white leather divan and black leather basket chairs. As a contemporary design the basket chair is one of the best, but its thin metal legs would seem to disqualify it for use on the rolling sea. This factor, however, evidently did not figure in any of the plans.

The dining tables, for instance, were set with china, silver and glasses, but had no outer ridges to keep the crockery from sliding off in heavy weather. I asked several salesmen about this and they said, "Oh, well, these people don't eat dinner until they're snugly tied up in the marina." Occasionally I spotted some relic from an earlier age of naval engineering, such as a rack to hold glasses or cups, but most of these eyesores had been eliminated.

I looked in the closets, expecting to find mops, brushes and the other usual tools of shipboard housekeeping. What I did find were vacuum cleaners and extra light bulbs. In many boats no nautical evidence remained except the steering wheel and instrument panel on the top deck, and I had the feeling that in a few years these would disappear, too. The engineers don't quite have the bugs out yet.

"Let's face it—it's a floating living room," said one customer as he looked around a typical interior, his eye

taking in the paintings, abstract lamps, flower arrange-
ments, fruit bowls, scatter pillows, bookshelves and whiskey
decanters. He wandered off downstairs (below) to see the
floating boudoir, which had imitation gold lamé bed-
spreads, a full-length mirror and an adjoining bathroom
with stall shower, monogrammed towels and bottles of
"guest soap."

There was every reason to provide for house guests on
these boats. Most of them, as the salesmen kept telling me,
"sleep eight." By the same token, they also eat eight, and
presumably there is no limit to the number that they drink.
In length they averaged between thirty and forty feet, and
their prices ran well into five figures. One forty-two-foot
cruiser sold for $55,000 on the third day of the show, and
it in turn was eclipsed by a forty-seven-foot launch priced
at $86,380, "including the perfume and the dogs," as its
dealer told me when I climbed aboard. The perfume I
found on a vanity in the master bedroom; the dogs were
two stuffed poodles in the children's room, and all else
was a suburban home-owner's dream come true. Fluffy
rugs, resting on foam rubber, yielded to the foot and
caressed the ankle. Air-conditioning maintained a benign
temperature, and over everything burbled soft music—
not sea chanteys, but the soothing instrumentals that bathe
so many restaurants and public lounges in America today.

"This is Muzak that can play for six hours straight," the
salesman explained, revealing a tape concealed behind a
panel. "It has speakers in the main saloon, in both state-
rooms and up in the pilot's chair."

Thus the head of the family need not be lonely at the
helm, while his loved ones luxuriate below, with nothing
to occupy his thoughts except the operation of the boat.
Music will help him forget that he is sailing. In fact, he
can even join his loved ones for a hand of bridge, setting

the automatic pilot and bringing downstairs a push-button device that will change the boat's direction in a crisis.

That these boats have all the comforts of home is because they have all the electricity of home: 110 volts. Dealer after dealer pointed out that the seafaring housewife can use all her customary appliances. Stoves, refrigerators and vacuum cleaners are hers for the flicking of a switch. So are TV sets, hot water and hot air.

No longer, needless to say, may a man buy a boat on his own initiative, simply because he likes the way it handles. Now he brings his wife around to feel the curtains and approve the decor, as any number of wives were doing at the boat show. "These drapes aren't nearly as attractive as ours," one said to her husband. "No," he agreed, "but I like these valances better."

She thought this over, and went on to a systematic pulling-out of drawers and poking-about in closets. Soon she was able to tell her husband exactly how she could arrange the boat to sleep six adults and two children, and eat them all. No questions were asked about the boat's engine. Quite possibly it didn't have one. The motorboat may now be entering the same phase in American life as the trailer, which has largely ceased to go anywhere, but remains dug into the secure soil of the trailer park.

To one woman, at least, the symbolism of home was very much intact. She went from boat to boat in search of new decorating ideas. "My boat is two years old and I'm eager to do it over," she told me, asking my opinion of a turquoise sofa where we had both briefly settled. "I just don't know," she said, "whether to make my sofa turquoise and keep the curtains gold, or to make the sofa gold and the curtains turquoise. My lampshades are coral red and the rug is beige, so I don't want to overdo it."

That was the closest that I came to feeling seasick at

the boat show. For relief I fled to the upper floors, where 400-odd dealers were exhibiting their wares. Again the boatmen went different ways according to their faith. Sailing buffs lingered at the booths of sailmakers and rope makers, or inspected new paints and finishes, or admired displays of marine hardware—the winches and cleats, blocks and pulleys, shackles and turnbuckles and other objects that satisfy the eye because long usage has ordained their particular shape.

Motorboat buffs browsed among the accessories, happy to come upon magnetized playing cards and self-balancing coffee percolators, cookbooks and shower curtains. They also found many dealers selling electronic navigators with such names as "transistor loran" and "depth-distance indicator," marvels that will detect "floating obstacles, submerged objects, approaching shorelines, other boats, docks, bottom contours and even schools of fish." (Up to now, bottom contours have been detected only on deck, usually in a tight bathing suit.)

With these devices the motorboat man need not keep his own lookout for pesky shorelines and other impediments to the proper use of leisure. He merely has to change course when his instruments tell him to. Even this inconvenience should soon yield to the swift march of American technology. Surely the day is not far off when instruments will both see and steer around the floating obstacle, the submerged object and the school of fish.

Then the boat owner and his family can go downstairs and enjoy television in peace, feet up, slippers on. If there should arise the horrid necessity of taking the boat from one marina to another, they don't have to watch. They can wait below until it's all over.

10. *Rope Lattimer, Come Out; or Eleven Personalities in Search of an Actor*

(After reading definitive magazine articles on Burt Lancaster, Jack Lemmon, Peter Sellers, et al.)

Go from table to table at any Hollywood bistro frequented by movie folk and ask "Who is Rope Lattimer?" and you'll be amazed at the different answers you get. You might think everyone would simply say that Rope Lattimer is the hottest film star in the business—because that's just what he is. Known to exhibitors as "Mister Box-Office" on the basis of his last three motion pictures, including the smash comedy hit, "Shower Curtain," with Doris Daybed, which ran a record thirty-seven weeks at Radio City Music Hall, Rope now commands a salary of $400,000 plus 10 percent of the gross, and producers are virtually pursuing him with blank checks. It is no secret, for example, that Otto Porringer has dangled a million-dollar percentage-and-participation deal before the ruggedly handsome star if he will undertake the triple role of Columbus, King Ferdinand and Queen Isabella in the psychological adventure yarn, "New World Symphony," due to go before the CinemaScope cameras next April on Lake Michigan. Rope is reported to feel that the script "isn't right for him," though he has no qualms about essaying the triple characterization.

"Myself, I'm nobody at all," he says candidly. "There is no Rope Lattimer. Not until I put on that costume and makeup do I flesh out into a believable person. People think they know me, but they don't. Nobody does. And that's because," he adds, tapping his chest for emphasis, "there's nobody here."

This is the fascinating irony behind Lattimer's meteoric rise, as I discovered when I went to interview him in his opulent new office on La Cienaga Boulevard. I had hoped to visit Rope in the seventy-two-room neo-stucco mansion with matching polo fields that he recently bought in swank Bel Air, where he lives with his wife, TV actress Peg Peignoir, her ten-year-old daughter Cerise, to whom Rope is devoted, and his own two boys by a former marriage, Rope, Jr., and Hemp, to whom he is devoted. Even in cynical Screenland this marriage is regarded as one of those rare idyls that will last forever, and Rope insists on keeping his home a private oasis where he and Peg and the kids can lead the life of a normal American family.

His office, on the other hand, can be seen—at least from the outside—by any passer-by in Los Angeles. A replica of the Petit Trianon, with the letters "R.L." embedded in the façade in semiprecious stones, the building gives every appearance of success and security. You enter through the lavatory, which is done in travertine imported from Tivoli and lined with twenty-four statues by Maillol; pass a swimming pool filled with naked starlets waiting for an appointment with Rope, who likes to do his own casting ("He's meticulous about every small detail of movie-making," says his long-time aide and sparring partner, "Pop" Farnsworth); wade through a shin-high rug made by dicing 15,000 perfumed letters from girls in the Rope Lattimer Fan Clubs that are mushrooming in every corner of the land, and come at last to the inner sanctum where Rope himself, attired in shantung pajamas flown in that morning from a tailor he owns in Kowloon, sits dabbing at a lunch of braised peacock, now and then idly flicking a piece of crabmeat with his salad fork onto one of the Rembrandts and Cézannes that surround his rhinoceros desk, which he personally shot two winters ago from his $75,000 air-conditioned lodge in the White Highlands of Kenya.

"Sure, I've got all this," he says, his arm describing an arc to embrace the countless material luxuries that have accrued to him in only six short years, "but what does it add up to? What do I add up to? There is no real me. I don't exist until I don somebody else's makeup and voice, and then that somebody else could be any of two or three dozen different characters."

I was fascinated by this apparent mystery. Was there really no man behind the legend? Or, if there was a man, who was he? I determined to find out, and I systematically queried his personal friends and associates. Oddly enough, however, the more I tried, the more elusive he became.

"Rope is a sweet, lovable guy," said his long-time production assistant and skin-diving partner, "Pop" Morse. "He's a real human being."

Yet the very next man I interviewed, Louie Laredo,

who directed him in the adult western, "Powwow at Pooscatuck," had an entirely opposite slant. "He's as mean a son of a gun as you'd hope to meet," opined Laredo. "Rope'd cut you dead for a one-sixty-fourth share of the popcorn rights."

I quoted these two contrasting views to Rope's long-time agent and skeet-shooting partner, "Pop" Twombly, and asked him which one was correct.

"Neither one," averred Twombly, and when he elaborated I found that his answer combined elements of both. "I wouldn't say he's a sweet, lovable guy. Don't get me wrong—I'm personally very fond of Rope. He's a real human being. But he's a highly complicated individual— nervous and irritable. Some days he'll snap your head off, but the next morning he's always sorry and he'll send over a new Ferrari or maybe a diamond stickpin. One thing about Rope is he's generous."

Similarly, there was no agreement on his personality when he is at actual work on a picture. "Such concentration you never saw," asserts his long-time dresser and gambling partner, "Pop" Nelson. "On the set he crawls into the skin of the character he's playing. I remember when he was doing Captain Flanagan, the skipper in 'Eighteen Years Before the Mast,' he got so immersed in the psychology of the role that I couldn't snap him out of it long enough for lunch. So one day I poured some beer over his head—Rope used to like that kind of kidding around when we were growing up in East Hoboken—and all he said was 'Bos'n, batten down the aft hatches, it's gonna be a wet night!' I tell you I'll never forget that episode."

However, when I queried Jill Organdy, his bosomy costar in "Monique La Triste," Billy Wildroot's chuckle-filled farce about a French streetwalker who breaks her leg and can't walk, she threw back her pretty auburn locks and laughed. "Oh, that Rope!" she trilled. "Is he ever a devil on the set! Always horsing around and hauling girls off to his dressing room! You never know if he's going to be ready for a scene or not. Half the time he can't remember what part he's playing or even what the picture is about."

Again I was struck by the diversity of views. Here were two people who knew him well and had toiled with him day after day in the grueling give-and-take of motion picture work. Yet they might have been talking about two separate men! I was confused, frankly, and it was not until I went to Rope's long-time tax expert and billiards partner, Si Zoomar, that a clear pattern emerged.

"In actual fact," declared Zoomar, "there are eleven different Rope Lattimers. He's played that many top-starring roles since 1958, and each one of them, in some strange way, is Rope himself." Zoomar went on to document his point with uncanny logic.

Lattimer No. 1 is proud and arrogant, the very qualities he brought to the screen as Flatulus, the Roman slave who converts to Christianity in "The Pontius Pilate Story." Says Zoomar: "That's the real Rope. Defiant! When he hit this crazy burg he wanted to show everybody!"

Lattimer No. 2 is humble and deferential, an exact ringer for Brother Brougham, the missionary to the Ububu tribe, whom Rope played in "These Were My Children." As Zoomar puts it, "There's a saintly quality about Rope that your average citizen would never suspect."

Lattimer No. 3 is proud yet humble, precisely the combination that he caught in "*Il Conte*" ("The Count"), Italian-made drama of a Venetian nobleman who united the haughtiness of his lineage with a self-abasing devotion to the peasants on his estate. "Anyone who knows Rope," points out Zoomar, "knows that that was a self-portrait."

Lattimer No. 4 is Madcap Rope, the happy-go-lucky clown of Billy Wildroot's chuckle-laden farce, "The Office," about a genial junior executive who pays for his secretary's abortion to get in good with his boss, though it turns out that he himself (and not the boss) was responsible for her comical condition. States Zoomar: "That's him all over— up to a lot of crazy tricks, but basically considerate."

Lattimer No. 5 is the lonely introvert, identical in every trait to his role in "Lizard Watcher of Leavenworth," the astonishing story of the convict who catalogued every known species of North American lizard in his clammy prison cell. "You might say that's his essential character," explains Zoomar. "More than anything else he wants to be left alone."

Lattimer No. 6 is the gregarious, outgoing kid who absolutely must be with other people. Cast as the jovial French commissioner of prostitutes' licenses in the afore-mentioned "Monique La Triste," he kept his fellow workers in stitches with his antics before the camera and between "takes." "He's fundamentally a happy guy," Zoomar claims. But when the other actors and grips left for the day, Lattimer would abruptly turn into:

Lattimer No. 7, an inherently melancholy man, who would sit at the piano on the empty sound stage picking out strange and rueful melodies until dawn. "Sad—that's what he is," says Zoomar. "It was like inspired to cast him in the title role of 'Gloomy Dane,' the filmusical of 'Hamlet.' Don't kid yourself it was any accident he was up for an Oscar for that performance."

Lattimer No. 8 is the lady-killer with a heart of ice. Significantly enough, the entire movie colony agreed it was a stroke of genius to cast him as the debonair private eye in "Dr. No-No," who charms pretty girls and then shoots them for fun. "That's the first role Rope really felt,"

Zoomar recalls. "He wasn't playing that detective—he *was* that detective."

Lattimer No. 9 is shy, serious and courtly with the opposite sex, the epitome of the diffident young social worker he delineated in "The Chadsey Report," Irving Walloon's scholarly analysis of wife-swapping in a well-to-do suburb of Galveston. This is "family man Rope," as Zoomar describes him, who loves to help his two boys with their homework and is a mainstay of the Bel Air P.-T.A.

Lattimer No. 10 is brassy "Big-Deal Rope," as he was dubbed during the filming of "12, 13, 14," Billy Wildroot's rib-tickling farce about an American tycoon who smuggles cookies through the Berlin wall for personal profit. "That was the genuine article—always out for himself," says Zoomar. "When his family wants help or his community asks him to serve on some board, he tells them off with a profanity that might surprise you."

Finally, there is Lattimer No. 11, who is very definitely an amalgam of the other ten: proud but humble, gregarious but antisocial, devil-may-care but constantly worried, gentle but hard, a Don Juan who quails in the company of women. Fusing these traits in his incisive portrait of Standpipe, the urbane plumber in "Shower Curtain," Rope achieved the finest feat of his career thus far. "He identified with Standpipe," explains Zoomar, and Doris Daybed agrees. "Acting opposite Rope," Doris told me, brushing away a freckle, "was a revelation. I saw for the first time that Rope is a very complex personality who remains, underneath, a very simple human being."

Now, in Lattimer's office, interviewing the star himself, I was grateful to Zoomar for having etched such a precise picture. How right the picture was, I thought, as I studied Rope's handsomely chiseled face. Playing across his features I could see a smile that kept merging, almost impercepti-

---

bly, into a sullen and hostile expression, and then back into a smile. His steely blue eyes radiated kindness, though deep in their pupils I detected a vicious cruelty. His strong hands were, for the most part, folded in the prayerful repose that one associates with priests and holy men; yet occasionally they would reach out to stroke the legs of a passing stenographer, and at other times, in a seizure of nervous energy, his fingers would crush into small bits an inkwell or some bronze memento on his desk.

"You're a strange man," I said, blurting out my puzzlement. "Who are you really?"

"Stop asking me that!" he replied, his warm and friendly voice edged with cold contempt. "How should I know? My father died two years before I was born. So did my mother. It wasn't easy growing up that way with no family, no roots. My only fulfillment is in my acting. Not until I put on that makeup do I flesh out into a believable person. The rest of the time I don't exist. There is no me—do you understand?"

His serene face began to quaver and became an indistinct blur. His body and his expensive clothes seemed to jiggle before my eyes as in a desert mirage. His normally low and mellow voice rose to an eerie, high-pitched tone which repeated, over and over, more faintly each time, until at last it died away altogether, the chilling words: "THERE IS NO ME! There is no me! *There is no-o-o-o-o me.*"

My eyes remained fixed on the mink chair where Rope Lattimer had been sitting during our interview. Suddenly nobody was there.

11. *What Ever Happened*
to Privacy?

THE EXACT MOMENT WHEN PRIVACY
began going out of American life has never been fixed by
scholars. Perhaps it was the day when Chic Young, creator
of "Blondie," first put Dagwood in the bathtub. Since then
countless children and dogs, trooping in and out of Dagwood's bathroom, have sailed little boats in the water
where he sat soaping. And countless real children (and
dogs) have copied the custom, assuming it to be common
behavior. Thus one of modern man's last sanctuaries has
been invaded and despoiled.

Invading other people's privacy is now a big pursuit—
and big business—in America. So is the voluntary surrender of privacy, judging by the large number of men
and women who seem driven to make an outward show
of their inner selves. Newspapers, magazines and television
programs are battening as never before on the personal

lives of the famous, and no detail is too intimate to be made public, as President Eisenhower found during his recovery from a heart attack. In fact, anyone who tries to guard his privacy is regarded as somewhat odd and un-American.

Certainly a man's home is no longer his castle, or, if it is, the moat is dry and the portcullis is always up. Nothing can stanch the daily tide of impersonal mail posing as personal mail, of salesmen at the door and strangers on the telephone. In the hands of the inconsiderate the telephone is a deadly weapon, but if a man dons armor against it by refusing to have his number listed in the directory, he must now pay a penalty. The New York Telephone Company has almost half a million of these diehards on its rolls—a figure which suggests that the urge for privacy is still alive, even if the respect for it is not. A few years ago the company became impatient with its unlisted patrons and put an extra charge on their monthly bill, hoping thereby to force them back into the listed world of good fellowship.

Modern architecture has also done its share to abolish privacy. The picture window was first designed by men like Frank Lloyd Wright to frame a scene of natural beauty. Today millions of Americans look out of picture windows into other picture windows and busy streets. The contractor has no sooner finished installing the picture window than the decorator is summoned to cover it with expensive curtains against an inquisitive world. Even then, privacy is uncertain. In many modern houses the rooms have yielded to "areas" that merge into each other, so that the husband trying to work in the "reading area" (formerly den) is naked to the blasts from the "recreation area" (formerly rumpus room) a few feet away.

If privacy is hard to find at home, it is almost extinct outside. Strangers in the next seat on trains and planes are seldom given to vows of silence, and certainly the airline pilot is no man to leave his passengers to their thoughts. His jovial voice crackles out of the intercom whenever the customers are in any danger of dropping off to sleep. Airplanes have also been infested by canned music, leaving the captive listener only one method of escape— and no method if he wants to live to tell the tale.

Unwanted music is privacy's constant enemy. There is hardly an American restaurant, store, railroad station or bus terminal that doesn't gurgle with melody from morning to night, nor is it possible any longer to flee by boarding the train or bus itself, or even by taking a walk in the park. Transistor radios have changed all that. Men, women and children carry them everywhere, hugging them with the desperate attachment that a baby has for its blanket, fearful that they might have to generate an idea of their own or contemplate a blade of grass. Thoughtless themselves, they have no thought for the sufferers within earshot of their portentous news broadcasts and raucous jazz. It is hardly surprising that RCA announced a plan that would pipe canned music and pharmaceutical commercials to 25,000 doctors' offices in eighteen big cities—one place where a decent quietude might be expected. This raises a whole new criterion for choosing the family physician. Better to have a second-rate healer content with the sounds of his stethoscope than an eminent specialist poking to the rhythms of Gershwin.

If Americans no longer think twice about invading the privacy of others, it is because popular example has demolished the very concept, as anyone with a TV set will attest. The past decade of television has been an orgy of prying and catharsis. Mike Wallace first achieved fame as a TV inquisitor who left no question unasked. To Drew Pearson, for instance, he said, "President Roosevelt once called you a chronic liar; President Truman called you an S.O.B. at one time and a vicious liar at another time. Could it be that you *are* a liar?" Wallace explained why such questions are tolerated: "People's thresholds are lower than they used to be."

Nor does TV fix its peeping eye only on the famous. Program hosts ooze familiarity, no matter who comes into their net, and sooner or later almost everybody does. How many wretched women were induced to bare their miseries on "Queen for a Day"? How many couples exposed their marital troubles to dissection on "Divorce Court"? Small legions allowed such retrospective shows as "This Is Your Life" and "It Could Be You" to conjure up spirits from their unhappy past. Dr. Joyce Brothers had a program on which she answered questions on the sexual problems of her listeners, and Jack Paar in his long tenure on the "Tonight" show frequently wheedled the audience's sympathy with tearful complaints about his personal woes. Who can forget his lachrymose return from exile after NBC suspended him? Jabbing at his various enemies, he had a special riposte for Walter Winchell, who, he said, had defamed him and even questioned his virility. "As a moral man," Paar declaimed, "only my wife knows about my virility," and with this touching domestic vignette he routed the foe from darkest Hearstland.

Even more symbolic of the new age was Ed Murrow's "Person to Person." In its seven years more than 550 men and women welcomed this program's 19 million viewers into their homes. They included four Cabinet members, two Supreme Court justices, three college presidents, three bishops, many visiting heads of government, foreign diplomats of highest rank, governors and mayors, Congressmen and judges, generals and admirals, one ex-President and one ex-King of England.

"It was very rare of people to refuse on the grounds that

it was an invasion of their privacy," says Jesse Zousmer, former producer of the show. "It became a question of prestige to be on it—sort of like being invited to the White House."

While TV programs thus invaded the privacy of men and women as a whole, TV commercials have gone after them limb by limb, and by now they have eroded most of the defenses that once surrounded the human body. When a toddler is old enough to turn a knob, he can see women flexing in girdles or "undies," or rejoicing in the thrust of a new brassiere. He can watch them spray deodorants or dab depilatories on themselves in a state of unaccountable rapture, or affix corn plasters to their tortured feet. Meanwhile, inside their transilluminated systems, little Mr. Aspirin is knocking at the door of the duodenum, Mr. Laxative is dutifully hurrying toward the colon, and Mr. Nasal Decongestant is flushing the eight sinus cavities.

In such an enlightened age, no wonder President Eisenhower's intestinal functions were front-page news. Three days after the President's heart attack James C. Hagerty told a news conference, "He had a good bowel movement," and Dr. Paul Dudley White hurried to explain why he had included this extraordinary detail: "The country will be very pleased—the country is so bowel-minded anyway—to know that the President had a good bowel movement this morning, and it is important."

Although assaults on privacy come from many sides, it is amazing how many are self-inflicted. Celebrities now disgorge their blackest secrets in print, as if hoping to banish their private demons by serving them at a public feast. From three such confessions an industrious scribe named Gerold Frank has mined one of the richest veins in recent literary annals. Frank is the ghost who put to paper Lillian Roth's "I'll Cry Tomorrow," Diana Barrymore's "Too Much Too Soon" and Sheilah Graham's "Beloved Infidel," books which together have sold 6 million copies and earned more than $750,000, including foreign editions and royalties from the movies that Hollywood avidly made from all three.

In their books Miss Roth and Miss Barrymore told explicitly how an overdose of husbands and liquor reduced them to squalid depths. "I told him things I wouldn't have told a priest," Miss Barrymore said, and Frank obviously had the same powers of exorcism over Miss Graham. In her book she confessed that her real name was Lily Sheil, which she loathed, and that her upbringing was far shabbier than the one she had invented to conceal it. "The whole of my childhood has been something dark and secret to me," she said, "and the name I was born with is tied up with the years I have kept hidden so long."

Miss Graham could have kept those years secret forever. They are her business, or at least they would have been so regarded in any era but this one, when there's no business like everybody's business. As for Frank, he moved on to Zsa Zsa Gabor, who promised to tell all, and "McCall's" had no doubt that she would, for the magazine paid $100,000 for the rights, thereby giving new momentum to the wave of confessional journalism that has made "McCall's" rich—and has forced competitors like the "Ladies' Home Journal" to throw dignity to the winds and join the profitable game of disrobing the great.

This undressing has even taken literal form. The mother-in-law of painter Larry Rivers once posed for him in the nude, and he exhibited the full-length portrait with the subject identified. During their marriage Tyrone Power and Linda Christian not only had themselves painted nude to the waist, but hung the portraits in their house and invited "Look" to publish photographs of them, which "Look" gladly did.

Such exhibitionism is not uncommon in people of artistic bent. What *is* uncommon is for a country's leaders to drop their mask in public and help a photographer perform a stunt, as dozens did in Philippe Halsman's "Jump Book." Halsman persuaded his renowned subjects—including Richard Nixon, Adlai Stevenson, J. Robert Oppenheimer, Learned Hand and John J. McCloy—to jump for him. "One of our deepest urges," he says, "is to find out what the other person is like." But could he have persuaded America's illustrious men to take to the air ten or fifteen years ago?

Perhaps the snooping instinct has been sharpened by the kind of magazine reporting that digs as deeply into a man as gall and tenacity will permit. "Time" boasts that its writers and researchers spend weeks trailing the subject of a cover story, detecting mannerisms that the subject's husband or wife never noticed. These techniques have undoubtedly inspired countless newspapermen, especially those who intrude on a family in their moment of grief after a tragedy. Sidney Skolsky is only being true to modern journalism's creed when he asks every Hollywood star if she (or he) sleeps in pajama tops, bottoms, or neither, and usually gets neither for an answer.

Serious writing has also suffered strange inroads. Before television, authors generally worked in seclusion while publishers tried to sell their books. Now it is necessary to sell the man as well as the book, and publishers try hard to get their writers onto "Today," "Tonight" and other shows moderated by popular hosts, who have thus become literary arbiters with considerable influence. Rare is the author, like J. D. Salinger, who refuses to undergo this kind of promotion. Meanwhile all sorts of entertainers have suddenly blossomed into "authors"—and best-selling authors, too. They go from show to show, touting their "books" and each other's books, which accounts for the success of these volumes, unaccountable by literary standards.

The decline of privacy coincides—by no accident—with the rise of the "public relations consultant," one of the high priests of modern American life. (Manhattan listed ten public relations firms in 1935; today there are at least 1,200 in the United States.) His original purpose was to knead the public image of his client, like a lump of clay, into a fresh and attractive shape. In some cases this means a lot of kneading, for he is often called upon to repair a reputation that was damaged almost beyond mortal help.

Today the function of the "p.r." man has grown far beyond these mere overhauls. Now the task is not so much to shine an image that has tarnished as to create one where none existed before. Hitherto faceless and nameless corporation presidents, bankers and other executives by the hundreds allow themselves to be converted into "personalities" by such puppeteers as Ben Sonnenberg, on the theory that a company is more lovable if its officers are, too. To help sell the man is to help sell the product.

One of privacy's last preserves used to be "Society," and it still is in most countries. Society is founded, after all, on the principle of excluding almost everybody else. "Not to attract attention to oneself in public," declared Emily Post, "is one of the fundamental rules of good breeding." This fundamental rule is still observed by those who already belong to the aristocracy—and is doggedly broken by those who are trying to get there, aided by the public relations consultant. Most ladies in this category now hire a press agent to get their name and picture into print as often as possible, and they invite the press to their private social affairs in such volume that they seem, judging by the subsequent accounts, to have invited none of their private social friends.

"I'm asked to many parties,'" says Eugenia Sheppard,

the New York "Herald Tribune's" lively columnist, "for no reason except that the hostesses expect me to write about them, and when I go I meet all the other fashion and society reporters." Certain ladies do indeed turn up with astonishing frequency in the New York papers, and it doesn't take a puzzle expert to locate them in print roughly once a day.

So far have the barriers fallen that Americans seldom think of invoking their moral and legal rights to privacy. As a people we are endearingly nice to strangers who pester us at the door or on the phone, apologizing elaborately for not doing what they so unfeelingly ask. We can rarely bring ourselves to ask a cab driver to turn off his radio or his voice. Not to call a man "Jim" or "Jack" from the first handshake is to sully the notion that we are all old pals together in the great Waring Blendor called America.

The legal case for privacy was eloquently stated by Louis D. Brandeis as far back as 1890, and his words are, needless to say, infinitely more pressing today: "The intensity and complexity of life, attendant upon advancing civilization, have rendered necessary some retreat from the world, and man, under the refining influence of culture, has become more sensitive to publicity, so that solitude and privacy have become more essential to the individual; but modern invention and enterprise have, through invasions upon his privacy, subjected him to mental pain and distress, far greater than could be inflicted by mere bodily injury."

Yet only rarely does a knight rise in full view to hurl back the enemy—so rarely that it is always a memorable moment when he does. One such moment was Randolph Churchill's reply to John Wingate when that TV interviewer asked a nosy question on his "Night Beat" program about "the arrest of your sister Sarah in California."

Churchill snapped: "I do not intend to discuss it with you. I never discuss matters relating to my family with total strangers. I wouldn't think of asking you about your sister. Why the hell should I let myself be bullied around and kicked around by you? Your shame is on your own head."

Equally stern was Steven Rockefeller's answer to reporters angry at being barred from his church wedding in a small town in Norway. "You represent the freedom of the press and I represent the privacy of an individual," he said. "To me this church service is a religious occasion and I am not a public figure."

What other oases of privacy remain? They can be almost counted on the fingers of a first baseman's mitt. One, paradoxically, is the commuter train. Though it is densely packed with men on its morning and evening journey, the man in the next seat occupies an inviolate island of silence, even if he is a close friend. Another oasis is the gentlemen's club. In that temple Emily Post brooks nothing but spartan self-control. "It is one of the unbreakable rules not to speak to anybody who is reading or writing," she says, and she might have added sleeping. "If a new member happens to find at the club no one whom he knows, he goes about his own affairs. He either reads, writes, or looks out the window, or plays solitaire, or occupies himself as he would if he were alone in a hotel."

Sometimes, in the strangling streets of Manhattan, a relic of privacy's golden age comes purring by and gives the heart a brief lift. It is a shiny cabriolet, its rear seat windowless and almost hidden from view. But in those dark shadows a bright object occasionally glitters. Is it the diamond choker of a very old lady going to tea with a girlhood friend? Is it the stickpin of a very old tycoon bound for his bank vault? Nobody on the sidewalk knows, and nobody ever will.

12. *Don't Look Now*

LIKE THE WEIGHT OF THE YO-YO (7.2 OZ.), the circumference of the muff (55 centimeters) and the specific gravity of the popover (0.82), the official length of the plunging neckline, as fixed by the Bureau of Standards after the famous Smilby alienation-of-affections case (Smilby *v*. Noodleberger), is so well known to the average American—5¼ inches, measuring from the collarbone— that I hesitate to mention it once again here. I do so only because it helps to explain my amazement at the fashion layouts that began to appear last fall illustrating the new styles, variously known as "The Plunge," "The V," "The

U," "The Split," "The Slash" and "The Scoop," which our women would start wearing in 1964.

Well, 1964 is here, and obviously we are all in for a nervous year. Any way you look at it—and almost any way is possible right now—the bosom is back on the national landscape. From the most fashionable evening dresses it looms into view, threatening total anarchy, held in check by the most tenuous margin and by what principle of physics no man knows—or should. As it is, we men are going to know more than ever before about the lady sitting next to us at dinner—or, more alarmingly, across from us.

Like any conquering army, the victorious bosom has been sending its alarums ahead for several months. I first noticed it—hardly proof of exceptional eyesight—in "Vogue" and "Harper's Bazaar," those august bastions of *haute couture*. It is not unusual, of course, for models to be displayed in those pages in varying stages of undress, but the purpose is never one of revelation. On the contrary, it is to prove how scientifically the American woman can be shored up by foundations, webs, struts and other tensile rods that might have been designed by Buckminster Fuller—a sight to thrill an engineer, perhaps, but not an ordinary liberal-arts type.

Here, however, were pictures by eminent fashion photographers like Richard Avedon and Irving Penn—men who can canonize any new style with the flick of a lens—of models who were anything but imprisoned. Their dresses dove to a point rather near the navel, leaving to the imagination only a little more than is left by "The National Geographic" when it visits one of those flagrantly feminine tribes of which it is so fond.

Newspapers also exerted themselves to spread the good news. "The American woman is ready to take the plunge," declared the oracular "New York Times." "The best continuous girlie show in town," said the New York "Herald Tribune," "is the spring fashion collections on Seventh Avenue. In every show there is at least one neckline slashed to forever." The paper amply documented its case with large photographs. One was of the finale of the Junior Sophisticates show, described in the caption as "bosoms all the way"—and bosoms all the way it was.

Another showed a "plunged *femme fatale* dress" designed by David Kidd of Jablow, and a third was a "slashed" black dress by Estevez, identified in the caption as a "*décolletage* expert"—which is nice work if you can get it, and Estevez has got it, for Eugenia Sheppard went so far as to call him "always the *décolletage* expert" in a column called "Acres of Skin." She was paying tribute to a dress by Estevez called "Blues in the Night," which was "slit to the waist, front and back."

She went on to mention a "snaky, black crepe evening dress with a low, low neckline" by Chester Weinberg, and then reported that Anne Klein "outdid Chester with a neckline that was wider and at least as deep." Clearly the great designers were engaged in a mighty contest, each goading his scissors on to new bursts of speed, like jockeys at the final turn, to win the Cleavage Sweepstakes, fashion's equivalent of the Kentucky Derby.

I'd put my money on Estevez; he doesn't sound like a man who would let himself be passed on the back stretch, and I fully expect to see a lady soon in an evening dress that Estevez has slashed to the floor. Then won't Chester Weinberg and Anne Klein be mad! Not for nothing has columnist Inez Robb gone on record that this is "the deepest, widest and most clinical cleavage in modern fashion history." Even bathing suits are to be cut low this summer—surely an extreme case of carrying coals to Newcastle.

At first glance (and also at second glance) this might seem to be an ideal situation for the American male, a new golden age—our overdue reward for all the recent years in which the designers have buttoned our ladies right up to the larynx. But at third glance I suspect that the game is going to make us uneasy and that we can't possibly win.

Obviously the new dresses have been plunged, slashed and scooped for our benefit. That much is certain—it is basic biology, as any schoolboy knows who has seen one paramecium wriggle to another. Therefore it follows that we are supposed to gaze at the semiexposed bosom with some sort of favorable attitude: admiration, or reverence, or plain old friendly respect. Anyhow, we are supposed to notice. In so doing we are playing our proper role of cavalier.

But we cannot notice too much, or too long. If we do, we play our other traditional role, of boor or lecher. Unluckily, the line separating the two is so thin as to be invisible. How much is too much? How long is too long? The man who knows this—who knows when the knight becomes the knight errant—is a man to be envied. He is bringing off one of the most delicate maneuvers in the battle of the sexes.

Perhaps there is no such man. For in this matter a woman will never give her admirer the benefit of the doubt. Counter to the judicial system that prevails elsewhere in America, a man is assumed to be guilty of bad intentions until proved innocent, and the only way he can be proved innocent, when confronted by a lady in a dress that has been "slashed to forever," is to wear a blindfold—or at least to spend the evening studiously examining the ceiling or the pictures on the walls. Never have the optical muscles been threatened with such a severe workout.

And this is not the only trap. There is also the question

of what a man should say. Assume he passes his initial test with gallantry. (I don't assume it for one minute, but I'm trying to think the problem through.) Assume that he enters a room and is introduced to one of the lady guests. He looks her in the eye as he greets her, and then glances briefly down to see her dress so that he can tell her that she looks lovely, as required by custom, whether she looks lovely or not. But where *is* her dress? Down, down, down go the eyes. The lady is definitely there . . . no doubt about that . . . but what can have happened to the dress? Good God! There's been a terrible mistake . . . oh, *there* it is . . . down by the abdomen. Thank heavens!

But he's not out of it yet. How do the eyes get back to the lady's eyes? If they return over the same hilly terrain, that's lechery for sure. Better to keep going down to the shoes and then make a wide circle, if possible to find a stiff drink, which should be gulped (a certain trembling of the hands is perfectly normal here), and then meet the lady's gaze again. The whole journey will seem to have taken an hour and will leave the traveler weak. His throat is dry, and yet he must find words. (His palms are wet, but that's no help.)

"You look lovely," he says at last. The familiar old words, always so safe, now seem positively lewd. Of course she looks lovely—there's more of her to look lovely. The lady smiles, sphinx-like, and says nothing, teasing her addled squire. She knows what he means by "You look lovely," and he knows that she knows that he doesn't merely mean "You look lovely." He's got to say something else—something about the dress. "Er . . ." he begins. In fact, every sentence he addresses to her thereafter begins with "Er." He tugs heavily on his drink, as if hoping to find his salvation there, to drain the proper phrase out of the enveloping gin.

"What a pretty dress!" he blurts out, finally, thinking as

it emerges that it's the stupidest remark he has ever heard. "I mean it's certainly very original. Made in Paris, I suppose? Oh. Estevez? I knew a guy named Estevez once. In the army. Morry Estevez. From Jersey City. Crazy little guy. I'll never forget one night Morry and I were on a patrol near Anzio, and the Jerries were throwing up a lot of ammo, and this crazy little Morry Estevez says to me . . ."

And so the boor turns into the bore, rambling down old military trails that don't even interest him, robbed of his senses like some punchy old boxer. He rivets the lady's eyes with a gaze as penetrating as an X-ray, desperate to keep his own eyes from wandering again to lotus land. At this point the lady would give anything to have the boor back. She will be pinned down outside Anzio for a good twenty minutes, as effectively as by machine-gun fire—caught, ironically, in a trap of her own devising.

Thus the year that promised to be so joyous, so full of snowy visions, will soon turn into the summer and winter of our discontent. We will simply not be able to stand the strain of engaging the ladies in this repeated test of nerves, this joust which challenges our manhood but pays off on good conduct. It is too much to ask.

If this were France—but it is not. I'm not complaining about the fact that it isn't France. I'm not even going to point out, as is the vogue in this age of psychoanalytical journalism, that we are all hideously repressed victims of an outmoded Puritan code. I'm merely stating that the ogle is not tolerated in this republic. The Four Freedoms stop short of that, and so does the Fifth Amendment.

So, Estevez, go home—and take David Kidd and Anne Klein and Chester Weinberg with you. Don't unbosom your sacred mysteries on us.

13. *Nobody Here But Us Sheep*

NEAR THE END OF "A STREETCAR NAMED
Desire," as every student of American folklore knows, the
loutish Stanley Kowalski carries the fragile Blanche DuBois
into his bedroom to a fate worse than death, as this form
of plunder used to be called, or, as it is known in modern
journalism, "criminal assault." In any case, it calls for a
certain initiative on the part of the male. Picture, therefore, a night several years ago when Ballet Theatre was
dancing this portion of the tale on the stage of the Metro-
politan Opera House. As the crucial moment approached,
Blanche (Nora Kaye) twirled to escape the lunging Stanley

99

(Igor Youskevitch). Suddenly, as he clutched at her, he fell at her feet and the curtain came down.

Those of us who were in the audience were momentarily puzzled, but within a few seconds we rallied and burst into the usual enthusiastic applause. Undoubtedly we all felt that, while this was not *our* conception of rape, the choreographer intended some symbolism that we were too stupid to understand, so we clapped heartily and pondered the subtleties of the artistic mind. Only the next day did we read in the newspapers that Miss Kaye, on her final twirl, had inadvertently clipped Youskevitch on the jaw and knocked him down for the count.

The story, though somewhat unusual in detail, is typical of the meekness with which Americans submit to the performing arts. We greet the right and the wrong, the good and the bad, with the same courteous warmth, and our entertainers rarely know when they have failed to entertain us. Basically this is a fine trait—it is politeness carried to an extreme that is positively Japanese. But it is also a surrender of control over our theatrical forms. The voice of protest is never raised in the holy temples where singers sing, dancers dance and mummers mum. An American will go to any length not to walk out of a performance or cause a fuss in public. Though dozens of poor plays and concerts and operas come to New York every year, the customers remain in their seats to the very end, as if bound by sacred vows. Under cover of darkness they may sleep— and countless husbands do—but they will not leave.

In Europe there is no such apathy about art. Passion runs high. The French and Italians do not hesitate to boo an errant troubadour, and even civilized England takes arms against dramas that fail to satisfy. When "The Connection" opened in London it was most uncivilly hooted off the boards. Peter Sellers recalls from his lean years that the toughest town on the British vaudeville circuit was Glasgow, where the Scots liked nothing so much as to pelt an English actor, and where a net was strung over the orchestra pit to protect the musicians from missiles that fell short of their human target.

It could be argued that Europe's performers are better for these periodic brushes with a discontented public, and that America's arts would be livelier if an occasional hiss or titter ruffled the chaste air. But such a heresy is unlikely. We have abdicated even the simple forms of dissent. One would think that when the audience filed back for the third act of a bad play, forty or fifty seats would yawn a silent protest at the actors. But the house is as full as ever.

Several factors hold the playgoer in this curious bondage. One is his feeling that the theater is a social event, a sort of party that he is obliged to attend. Women are the main conspirators in this fiction. Many a man, tempted to leave, has been told by his wife not to "make a scene." Besides, wives have a touching faith, totally unsupported by the facts, that in the last act "it's going to get better." The playgoer also feels that he must stay to get his money's worth. He has paid a huge sum for tickets, baby-sitter, drinks and dinner, and he is determined to enjoy himself. To leave in the middle, he thinks, is to ruin the evening that he has dearly bought.

On the contrary, it is the only way to save what he has dearly bought. By remaining he voluntarily exposes himself to boredom, pain and mounting rage against the producer, playwright and actors. If he leaves he can still catch the movie that he wanted to see in the first place, or hear a new night-club singer, or seek some other "attraction" that really attracts. This means spending a little more money, but for sheer therapy it is money well spent. There is almost no moment so exhilarating as the one when a defector strides out of an auditorium that has become a cave of stale winds. The air in the street is fresh with freedom.

It is in the concert hall that we are at our most docile. Every year horrid musical experiments are inflicted on the faithful. Electronic compositions, for instance, which make use of sirens, rattling chains, lions' roars and other unpleasant noises send listeners out reduced to piteous moans —but not until the concert is over. Even the non-electronic composers, the mere twelve-tone modernists who use ordinary instruments, achieve sounds that fall harshly on the ear.

Unluckily, the serious music lover is up on his musical history. He knows that the composer is always ahead of the layman, and that many works which sound bland today were once thought hopelessly dissonant. He is resolved not to be a chump in his own generation, so he sits through the weird concerts, which often emanate from many distant corners of the hall, puzzling out the program notes and applauding briskly at the end.

The problem, of course, is to distinguish between honest experiment and quackery. We want our conductors to lead us into new territory and to stretch our horizons. On the other hand, we don't want to be used as guinea pigs just because we are too timid to grumble. A prankish conductor would have no trouble hoaxing us with a concerto for steam radiator or combustion engine.

Much can be achieved by sincere protest. A philippic delivered in mid-performance, or a shoe hurled in anger, would remind the producers, impresarios and theater owners that we are still around. As things stand, they have every reason to regard us as sheep and to give no real thought to our needs once they have taken our money. Surely it is time to cry our resentment against all the trite comedies that reach Broadway every season simply because they can be sold in advance to "benefit audiences" on the basis of a star's name, and can therefore obtain a theater. Strong action might bring a few plays to town on the basis of originality or merit. Another value of protesting—whether we leave a play or concert, or write letters about poor movies and TV programs—is that we retain our critical faculties. These have atrophied through lack of exercise, even though it is the historic function of the audience to shape its own diet.

Perhaps this will be the year of revolution. Perhaps, in some dark theater, when some wooden hero says to some vapid heroine, "How can I make you understand?" a lone freedom fighter will rise in his seat, shake his fist at the performers, shout his opinion of the whole dreary charade, and stalk out. It's just possible that the entire audience will get up and follow him, that the entire nation is secretly yearning for such a leader.

14. *Far Out on Long Island*

THE TWO-CAR GARAGE, LONG A SYMBOL OF the American dream to have two of everything, from cars to TV sets to refrigerators, is losing status as a symbol. Now the big thing is to have a second home—a house in the country for weekends and vacations—and countless city-dwellers are making the dream come true. More leisure enables them to escape the city for longer periods; easy credit enables them to buy a rural retreat by the mere deposit of their name on a friendly blank form; and new expressways abridge the miles to places that were once too many hours away. The result is a whole new wave of settlers pushing into summer colonies that used to be the preserve of the rich or the idle, imposing new patterns of architecture and conduct. Nowhere is the movement so intense or so full of variety as among the families—many of them artists and other creative folk—who leave New York every Friday and point their cars toward the Montauk Highway.

Unlike the yellow brick road that meanders through Oz, the Montauk Highway does not lead to an amiable wizard. It is not even a proper highway; it is full of jagged turns where a driver least expects them. But to those who follow it out the remote southern fork of Long Island it has definite magic powers.

The motorist is more than ready for magic after driving almost two hours across Long Island's dreary interior, and when he reaches the Highway his spirit quickens. Salt air reactivates a nose deadened by urban fumes. Small roadside stands with crudely lettered signs—BAIT, FLOUNDER, STEAMERS, LOCAL VEG—remind him that food comes from the sea and the soil and not from the supermarket.

The homes have no hint of Suburbia or of the glossy Exurbs. This is the look of rural America: the people are small-town merchants or truck farmers or fishermen, and many of their houses are several hundred years old, plain shingled buildings that survive from the early English settlers. As final proof that the city is now far behind, duck farms sprawl along the successive inlets, each an infinity of white feathers. Obviously "roast Long Island duckling," that hardy staple of the American hotel menu, is in no danger of dying out.

Revived by these verities, the driver hurries on to the particular town that is his chosen oasis for weekends and summer vacations. It may be quite near, if the town is

Westhampton or Quogue. It may be an hour farther if the town is Southampton or Water Mill or Sag Harbor, and it will be still more if it is East Hampton, Amagansett or Montauk Point itself, where the highway at last defers to the ocean. Long Island is more aptly named than most people think. The glamorous "Hamptons," bunched together in popular fancy, are actually scattered across forty miles.

Nor is geography all that divides them and their satellite villages. In social structure and attitude they are as different as cummerbund and hula shirt, and each is a zealous guardian of its own codes of privacy and familiarity, dress and undress, tolerance and intolerance. Some have become cells for painters or writers or theatrical folk, and so have sprouted chichi shops on Main Street and glass houses in the surrounding fields. Others have tried to hold the line— to preserve their identity as bastions of the Old Guard— against the tide of new settlers. But the tide is getting bigger every year. To be far out on Long Island is now very much in, and when the city-dweller finds his second home there, even if it is only a shack, he becomes its champion and slave.

Every Friday evening, in a car distended with portable cribs, portable babies and other familial gear, he leaves New York and hurtles to outer Long Island, drawn to his goal as obsessively as any pilgrim. On Sunday night, broiled by the sun, washed externally by the ocean and internally by gin, he bundles his cranky children into the car, hopeful that by starting early he will "beat the traffic," and turns his headlights westward for the long voyage home, one which doesn't beat the traffic and which never seems to end.

Such a trip, repeated so often, ought to blunt the strongest passion. Yet the call of outer Long Island continues to drown out the voices of logic and gloom. Those who keep answering the call, week after week, do so for different specific pleasures, but they are all joined in the belief that the area has a special feeling that they would not find anywhere else.

Essentially it is a feeling of openness. The terrain is flat and its most congenial crops are those which don't grow high enough to block the view. Potatoes are obviously the most congenial of all—potato fields, distinctively green, stretch away for miles, their linear pattern broken only by a random house or windmill. It is not a view for anyone who wants his scenery to be spectacular. This is a landscape of subtle charms.

Yet many new settlers would rather build beside a potato field than beside a beach, and it is not hard to see why. A driver who turns off the Montauk Highway onto the smaller roads that interlace these fields will soon succumb to their repose and their austere beauty. Perhaps only the interior of New England has this Early American quality, and there no water enlarges the view.

On outer Long Island, water is always near and often in sight. Sometimes it lies beyond a potato field: pale blue tacked onto pale green. It is not necessarily the ocean. Behind barriers of sand the ocean has formed, and the Indians have largely named, Moriches Bay and Quantuck Bay, Shinnecock and Mecox and Peconic Bay, and many other gentle bodies of water which are all things to all sportsmen—to the swift water-skier and the stuck clam-digger—and are equally kind to experts and beginners, old and young.

A boy learning to sail can own the water, and so can his sailboat-racing father who already knows how, and so can their natural enemy, the motorboat man, that urban admiral who goes from one marina to another on Saturday afternoon, playing cards on the deck as if he had never left home. Novice fishermen will catch as many snappers as the old pro. Luck favors those who haven't particularly earned it, and this is all the assurance that the newcomer needs.

Hearing of the bounty of the bays, passing stores that sell marine equipment, seeing small boats being towed on trailers to the sea, he soon stops thinking of the water as alien territory. It becomes an extension of himself and of his attainable world. He buys a boat and begins going for rides as habitually as he used to take his family out in the car. He learns the release of putting out from land, symbol of his weekday woes, and looking back at it in tranquillity, briefly beyond the reach of bosses, bankers, relatives, headlines, unwashed dishes and other mortal coils.

But of course it is the ocean that gives outer Long Island its true extra dimension. If oceans vary in beauty according to the shore that they meet, the Atlantic can hardly be more beautiful than it is here, for it breaks onto a smooth white beach that appears to have no limit in either direction. Though countless summer houses now perch on its dunes, though bathers swarm over it from June to September, they scarcely make a dent on the vast purity of the shoreline. Even people who live a few miles inland are subject to its elemental power. They don't like to let a day elapse without driving down to see and hear and smell the ocean, to savor its changing patterns and colors, and often, toward evening, they do.

If it is a violent ocean, so much the better—high winds make the sea, if anything, more hypnotic and beautiful. Outer Long Islanders have known many such seas in their hurricane-tossed lives. Their recent folklore abounds with storms named Carla and Donna and Ella, and the evidence is still strewn before their eyes—an icebox, perhaps, or a bathtub left naked on the sand by a wave that washed away the house that it was in.

One of these houses still sits in Moriches Bay, a memento of the 1962 storm that severed the Westhampton dune, and at least its whereabouts are known. Fifty others vanished completely, borne out of sight but not, needless to say, out of mind for the people who owned them. Here nobody forgets that the gods of wrath are still mightier than the gods of realty. A man whose house overlooks the beach may ostensibly have his eye on the steak that he is barbecuing, or on the bikini wiggling by. Actually his eye is on those dark clouds forming in the West.

Onto this natural playground the new settlers have grafted their playhouses in every conceivable and inconceivable shape. Their impact on some communities has been heavy; on others they make almost no mark. It depends on whether the town fathers want to save their original character or bend their zoning laws to catch the summer trade.

Nowhere have the invaders been embraced more avidly than in Westhampton. This is the nearest of the far-out colonies and its beach is the most breathtaking. Consequently, unlike the farther-out towns which appeal to artists and writers who are in no great hurry, it attracts the feverish folk of Broadway, movies, TV, advertising and publicity. As speed is their mainspring and sun-worship their summer religion, they find Westhampton ideal for its proximity and climate. Quitting work on Friday night, they hop into their sports cars—curled beside them are the ladies with whom they will be spending the weekend, who quite often are their wives—and roar out from Manhattan to the houses that they have built on Dune Road.

These houses, quite close together, appear to sit in mid-air. They are on stilts, theoretically safe from high seas that might crash over the dune, and each is a novel projection of ramps and decks which enable the owner to bask in the sun all day, clad in a bathing suit, playing Scrabble and listening to LPs of Broadway shows, without going near the water. Along this road a half-dozen huge hotels, boatels, night clubs and cooperative apartments have also been allowed to rise, ugly leviathans that dwarf their simpler surroundings.

Traffic, as a result, is fast and fierce, day and night, as the beach-dwellers go to each other's houses for parties or into the village for provisions. The village of Westhampton Beach, ordinarily small and sleepy, turns in summer into a miniature Miami, a continuing display of beachwear in all the colors of the rainbow and many more. Fey little art galleries and specialty shops bloom for three months between the butcher, the plumber, the electrician and the general store, patronized by women in cerise toreador pants, high-heeled sandals and sequined dark glasses of enormous size—acquaintances in New York but unrecognized by each other in all this casual panoply. Radios blare out of open Jaguars, and the talk on the sidewalk is of "picture deals" and box-office grosses. In various pockets of the village the old residents retain their oases—their country club, beach clubs and staid houses—but it is not the same place where they first planted their flag and sank their spiked golf shoes a generation or two ago.

The adjoining village of Quogue, by contrast, recently celebrated its 300th year and still looks like that kind of town. Its wide and tree-lined main street is as serene as Westhampton's is not, and along its side roads are dozens of brown shingled houses, big and roomy and ringed with porches, that uniquely spell "summer colony" in the American East. If Quogue lacks the vitality of its neighbor, it has a compensating beauty and peace. And if a deep peace has also settled over its ideas and opinions, that is the price that such dynastic resorts pay—and are glad to pay—for stability in a time of change.

No Long Island resort is as dynastic, however, as Southampton, a half-hour farther on, beyond Hampton Bays and the Shinnecock Canal, which the Indians called "Canoe Place" and which is still thick with boats, and beyond the reservation where the Indians still live and hold an annual powwow. These Shinnecocks are obviously the first families of Southampton, though the English made a good run for getting there early, as their clapboard houses, dating from the mid-1600s, attest.

But it is the current families who give the impression of having owned the town forever. Their big and pretentious mansions exude the very essence of accumulated wealth—they are set on vast estates, approached by long driveways, guarded by ornate portals, and encircled by hedges so impeccably trimmed that their care must occupy the entire corps of local laborers from May to October. There is something forlorn about these stone palaces that trail off into servants' wings for servants who no longer exist, immense ghosts from the age of Gatsby, outmoded by time and taxes.

Their owners nevertheless continue to fight the good fight. Lawn tennis is still maintained in the grand manner at the Meadow Club; the patriarchal Bathing Corporation is still the sole answer to that curious question, "Where do you bathe?," and the after-dark amusements, judging by the local columns, still invoke the desperate gaiety of the jazz age, tinctured by only an occasional hint that the atom has been split: "Mr. and Mrs. Francis T. Hunter held a lively party in their 'El Morocco' bomb shelter on Friday that lasted into the wee-small hours."

When the Southampton folk emerge from these various warrens it is usually to go shopping and rub elbows of bright silk and cashmere in Job's Lane. This short street manages to compress many of America's most expensive clothing salons, antique dealers and other sellers of elegant baubles. Only a few yards away, by coincidence, is the Southampton historical museum, which contains some of America's oldest, rudest and most utilitarian objects. Thus the genteel millionaire also rubs elbows with his fibrous ancestor—an encounter not to be missed.

It is because Southampton is such a cul-de-sac that the new settlers have pushed right past it to the wide-open potato fields, uncluttered dunes and liberal winds of Water Mill, Bridgehampton and Sagaponack. The very openness of this region is its best defense against conformity. The houses are dispersed widely, wherever a city-dweller has been able to buy a few acres from a potato farmer, and they are as different as their owners. Some are old barns which artists have converted to their use; some are new geometric forms, mostly of glass, which architects have raised for themselves and their venturesome clients.

To call this area an artists' "colony" is not strictly true. It is not compact enough. Nevertheless a growing number of artists, musicians, writers and editors live here, and anyone who wants to talk shop will find his man within ten miles—or his woman, for many of these marriages were made, if not necessarily in heaven, at least on Parnassus. The composer composes while his wife paints, and when the literary critic takes a wife she is often a lady novelist.

In only one of the far-out towns are the new settlers wholly invisible: Sag Harbor. Quite a few artists and writers have bought houses in this old whaling port, but it is clear that they chose the town for what it was and not for what they could make it into. Its main street is the most purely American, with a red brick municipal hall built in 1846, and it has not changed much since the days that are glorified in its whaling museum. It has no chic shops, and, as one artist said, "Nobody would use them if it did."

Still farther on, the Montauk Highway turns abruptly into one of America's prettiest towns. At first glance the spacious main street of East Hampton, divided by a broad common and a pond, flanked by historic houses, terminating in an ancient windmill, looks almost "restored." All, however, is genuine; the village has simply kept the shape that its original settlers fixed in 1648.

Newer settlers have long been lured by its charm and its fine ocean beach, and as these "summer people" were mainly members of the Old Guard they have made East Hampton into the most posh of the far-out towns. Their houses have the studied simplicity of the aristocratic rich. Their club, the Maidstone, a monolith of golf courses, swimming pools, beach cabanas, ballrooms and bars, sits on a hill like a Tudor manor and dominates the residential section in more ways than one. East Hampton society falls into two distinct groups: those who belong to Maidstone and all the rest.

As this is not the chummiest arrangement, the very new settlers—particularly those of creative bent—have fanned out to nearby villages of less formality, where Bermuda shorts are not a required uniform, such as Amagansett, or have staked out local beaches of their own. The busiest of these, the "Coast Guard beach," is popular with theatrical producers and playwrights. In fact, a faithful reader of the Broadway columns is led to believe that half the plays in any season originate when Producer X, emerging from the surf, spots Songwriter Y under an umbrella, recognizes Dramatist Z coming over the dunes with his crossword puzzle, sees Director A playing volley ball with Ingenue B, and signs them all to do a musical that has just occurred to him, with the help of Lady Agent C, who pops providentially out of the sand at that very moment.

Only one far-out town is really an artists' "colony"—an odd little settlement three miles out of East Hampton called The Springs, and it is not a town at all. Served only by a tiny grocery store and a gas pump, it consists of a lonely road that wanders through field and scrub with sporadic houses on either side. They are nondescript old farmers' houses, and nobody would suspect that they now belong to important artists, who have kept the plain exteriors and streamlined the rooms inside.

Jackson Pollock, fleeing the hostile New York art world, came to this isolated spot in 1946, and gradually other painters followed. As Pollock's work at last caught on, and especially after his death in 1956, the colony became almost a shrine, and so did the Pollock house where his widow, Lee Krasner, still lives and paints. Today the abstract expressionists in The Springs form a sizable clique, and they do not lack for admirers—East Hampton is full of wealthy patrons and hangers-on who love to give "twist" parties for the painters and thereby crash their world.

"After a while," one young artist says, "some of these party-givers even start painting—and then of course we drop them."

Having no beach of their own, the artists of The Springs use the Coast Guard beach in East Hampton, but not for inspiration. In this they are unlike all the other creative folk who have settled in Long Island's far-out towns because the wild beauty of the landscape is a direct or indirect influence on their work.

"We bring our image out from New York," says one abstract expressionist, "and that's what we paint. The other day a group of us were down at the beach, talking, when a lady came along with a paintbox, and do you know she had the audacity to sit down and paint the ocean."

So heavily do the city-dwellers imprint themselves on the rural landscape during June, July and August that it is hard to conceive of a time when they will go away again. Summer's lease, Shakespeare notwithstanding, has all too long a date—or so the serious artists of the region would say. They can hardly wait for Labor Day weekend, when most leases expire and they are left in peace.

On the day after Labor Day they awaken to a quiet that is almost primordial. The last transistor radio has gone crooning back to Manhattan, and not a single MG remains to terrorize the roads. The local newsdealer has stopped selling "Variety"—talk has consequently shifted from the turkeys of far-off Broadway to the potatoes of the farmer next door.

The Long Island Railroad's daily "Cannonball," a faithful if somewhat misnamed train, which has been a rolling houseparty all summer long, bringing out from New York every Friday afternoon a steamy tangle of seersucker coats, cotton dresses and new-strung tennis racquets, is back to normal length and personality, shorn of the extra Pullman cars that the line adds in warm weather to coddle, or at least anesthetize, its richer riders.

Even nature conspires to set the day after Labor Day apart from all others. By coincidence, or perhaps by some mystical law, it is invariably a day of such clarity as to wash the land clean and announce its renewal. Outer Long Islanders boast that autumn, not spring, is the best time of year, and they are right. There is a pinch in the air and a brilliance in the sky, and the water is of a blue so pale that it almost ceases to be blue. Anyone who walks on the beach, now swept of summer's traces, will share it only with the birds stopping off on their southward flight. Otherwise it is as near to solitude and serenity as many people manage to come.

This is when the various artists of far-out Long Island,

staying on, really get down to work, when presumably their muses are most propitious. The novelist writes with fresh vitality, the critic's vision is as clear as the atmosphere around him. The poet's well of imagery, brackish all summer, is suddenly replenished and pure. The composer hears no dissonant note, and even the abstract painter, who claims immunity to his environment, sees taking shape on his canvas a pattern whose tensions are slightly less tense than usual.

If this is not necessarily a good thing, if these are currents that the artists do not want to see in their art, they can repair the damage overnight by returning to the anxious city. With every year, however, they seem less and less impelled to do so, which would suggest that in their gradual colonization of this spacious land they have found —and founded—a real "artists' colony" after all.

15. *"Dig We Must"*

PROFESSOR PLONK, THE GREAT COLUMBIA
archaeologist, hit on his bold scheme in the spring of 1958.
He was sure that the richest of all Indian remains lay beneath the pavement of Manhattan, but there was no way
of getting at them. Certainly he could not expect the city
officials to cooperate. He had to devise a more subtle way
of poking through the asphalt crust without arousing suspicion.

Enlisting the help of the Columbia engineering faculty,
he began digging one morning at Fifth Avenue and 58th
Street—a crowded intersection, to be sure, but one which

he thought was directly over an old Indian settlement. He brought to the site many special tools that he and his students had made. This included some iron railings and wooden saw-horses on which they had painted "Dig We Must—for Growing New York." Dr. Plonk's assistant, Dr. Plink, had the happy inspiration of painting these saw-horses orange, that being the official color of the city.

Traffic began to clog nicely, as cars and buses maneuvered around the diggers in their little enclosure, but no driver stopped to protest. Within an hour Dr. Plonk had breached the surface and was down to eight feet. There he put into action a machine which he had built in the engineering laboratory—a combustion device that blew huge gusts of steam out of the hole and into the faces of strollers and bystanders. The students took turns cranking the steam machine, for Dr. Plonk insisted that it be going at all hours. He also deployed three or four students to sit up on the street eating sandwiches, drinking coffee out of thermos bottles and exchanging ribald jokes. Occasionally they were supposed to whistle at a pretty girl.

Meanwhile Dr. Plonk groped through a maze of pipes and ganglia to reach bedrock. Every morning he sent two students up from the hole with a tangle of wires, which he had brought along for this purpose. They unraveled the wires for several hours, while pedestrians watched with rapt attention, and then braided them back together. The two students became so good at this that they did it every day for three months, achieving not only some intricate wire patterns but some unusually crude banter about the racetrack and the "broads" they had known in the army overseas.

Below, in the gloom, Dr. Plonk and his graduate students came upon their first artifacts. These were Dutch utensils which he dated to a factory in Delft, circa 1500. He was quite annoyed to find them, actually, for he was in search of older civilizations. Nevertheless he dutifully photographed and indexed every scrap, and at night he brought these items up from the depths in a bag marked "Consolidated Edison." It was not until the third week that he struck his first trace of Indian life. To follow it further would mean tunneling southward in the direction of Tiffany's, and that of course meant widening the hole up on Fifth Avenue.

Luckily the steam machine and the conduct of his students made the operation look so official that nobody had asked any questions, and he was emboldened to branch out. He dug a trench past the Bergdorf-Goodman windows toward 57th Street and had his helpers build a wooden catwalk for the pedestrians. The people used these shaky bridges obediently, and Dr. Plonk began to wonder how far the patience of the public could be tried. One day he built a little wooden stile, for no reason at all, but the pedestrians went up one side and down the other without a whimper. They didn't even look down into the hole.

This proved to Dr. Plonk that he could get away with anything, and he eagerly assigned his staff and students to open new excavations all over the city. He chose the sites from clues he had found on an Algonquin potsherd under Van Cleef & Arpels. These sites were in congested sections of Manhattan—two were in the garment district, three were in the side streets which feed over to Broadway and jam so badly at theater hour, and one was at Columbus Circle. But Dr. Plonk didn't care. He was caught up in a strange exhilaration, and he made plans that were even more ambitious.

One month he had a bad scare when the newspapers printed a flurry of letters complaining that half the streets in New York were torn up. But no action was ever taken.

A few letters also growled that the temporary covers over the holes were noisy. This was something that Dr. Plonk could not avoid. He had to close the excavations from time to time, while he catalogued his findings in the Columbia lab, and the engineering faculty never managed to fit those lids well. They rattled fearfully, especially in the night.

But this was no reason to stop the work, for Dr. Plonk was now well below the Indian strata and into still older cultures. He discovered a Stone Age village under the Cort Theater, which made things quite sticky on matinee days, and he created a nasty traffic knot in Times Square when he unearthed some bones as old as the Neanderthal Man.

With this discovery Dr. Plonk knew that he had found his life work. All Manhattan must now fall under his spade. To recruit more helpers he revealed his secret to the dean of archaeology at New York University, who willingly joined the dig. That was in the fall of 1962. Now, at least 100 city blocks are estimated to be open with holes of various sizes, and on quiet days the muffled sound of pick and shovel can be heard far below.

16. Is It True What the Movies Say About . . . ?

IN THE YEAR 1958, WHEN GOOD QUEEN Bardot ruled the movie world and it was hardly worth exposing a film unless the star was exposing her body, a curious bit of surgery took place. An American movie exhibitor received from Sweden a picture that he had agreed to release in this country. To his horror, it contained no nude bathing scenes.

There was only one thing to do, and he did it. He found some nude bathing scenes elsewhere and spliced them into the movie at points where the action seemed to lag. Thus he gave his film what the trade calls a "hypo." For it is a law of economics that a movie prospers in direct ratio to the number of maids who disrobe while the plot runs its course.

This probably was not the exhibitor's motive. I think he was merely trying to achieve an authentic portrait of Sweden, which this movie obviously was not. For anyone who has seen a Swedish film knows that nude bathing is common, perhaps even compulsory, in that land. The ones that I have watched were all bleak and Gothic tales, but in each case I was pleasantly surprised to see the young lovers slip out of their civvies and into a silvery lake as casually as if they were stopping for a malted at the corner drugstore.

Why the travel agents don't publicize this aspect of Scandinavian life I can't imagine. They never get through to me, somehow, with all their talk of fjords and reindeer herds, but I'd gladly stop off for a few days in any country where the girls don't believe in bathing suits. I can only conclude that, since travel agents don't overlook the smallest "point of interest"—no matter how uninteresting it really is—nude swimming is actually not a Swedish custom, and the nation's movies do not reflect the nation's habits.

But does any country create a true portrait of itself on film? In France, if its movies are any index, no husband would dream of going home to his own bedroom at night. A far stronger instinct takes him to the boudoir of his mistress, a worldly beauty of the type that composes half the population of Paris. If he did go home that would be the last place to find his wife, for she steals off every afternoon to comfort some handsome young devil like Gérard Philipe.

Of course I may have the wrong impression of France, too. Conceivably there are millions of husbands and wives who love each other. It may be possible to walk the full length of the Riviera and not see a Brigitte Bardot changing from her street clothes into a bandanna, or even a Band-Aid. But the world sees France through her movies, and in this mirror a land of eternal revels is reflected.

If you are not looking for pagan pleasures, the place to go is Great Britain. Now there's a country with charm. Most of the men are whimsical chaps like Alec Guinness, who dabble in robbery and homicide but do it in such a funny way that you can't help liking them, or antic villagers of the kind who hid the whiskey in "Tight Little Island," or jolly manor lords who talk of cricket so amusingly that they sound like Noel Coward or Oscar Wilde.

Most of the other Britons fall into a second category. They are the officers who go off to their fate with a nonchalance that only centuries of breeding can mold: "I shouldn't wait up if I were you, Pam—Jerry may keep us busy for a few days." Pam herself, who guesses the truth— that her husband is going to swim underwater into Hamburg with a bomb in his teeth—smiles bravely and says, "Cheerio, Nigel; don't fret about me and little Robin— we'll all be together for the weekend, you'll see."

I began crying over this kind of thing in "Cavalcade" and haven't stopped yet. Only lately have I begun to see English films in which the stiff upper lip turns soft, in which the British Isles are revealed to have some seamy citizens as well—films like "Room at the Top," "Saturday Night and Sunday Morning," "A Taste of Honey" and "This Sporting Life." In such unsentimental tales the English are coming close to catching the real temper of English life.

But these films are still only a trickle in the larger flood. Besides, the characters are generally Cockneys or Yorkshiremen who speak a language seldom identifiable as the mother tongue. (One exhibitor recently put English subtitles on an English movie that he was importing to America.) This makes the film sound so alien, a product of some country like Bulgaria, that it leaves unsullied my vision of Britain as the ideal blend of droll spirit and noble heart.

Italy, in the years after the war, came closest of all to capturing the truth about itself on film. Several directors, notably Roberto Rossellini and Vittorio de Sica, made movies of heartbreaking honesty, such as "Open City," "Paisan," "Shoe Shine" and "The Bicycle Thief." They didn't build sets; they simply took their cameras into the streets, and for stars they chose ordinary people who looked right for the role. The resulting films were a poignant study of men, women and children caught in the tides of war and the rubble of peace.

But these movies were too true for the Italians, who shunned them at the box-office, not caring to be reminded of what they already knew. Italy's movie industry quickly began making movies that the people really wanted to see. They were breezy fables full of tinsel and glitter that didn't represent the country but did gratify the popular appetite for escapist fare. Through these films such ripe lasses as Gina Lollobrigida and Sophia Loren rose to fame and fortune. De Sica went back to acting, his original métier, and hasn't done much directing since. When he does, the picture has his customary stamp of humor and humanity, but such pictures don't emerge often from Italy. The director who comes closest to matching De Sica's art and compassion is probably Federico Fellini. His early successes— notably "I Vitelloni," "La Strada" and "Cabiria"—had a sure touch of truth. Since then, however, Fellini has sought his truth in the trickier mirrors of irony or allegory, as in "La Dolce Vita," and though the results are always interesting, they have an inflated quality that puts them just beyond common grasp.

Many countries, though they fail to reflect their present,

do a glorious job of etching their past, which is conveniently vague and can be decked in all the robes of chivalry and romance. The American western, for example, endows its sheriffs and cowboys with the most sterling virtues, and even the goodhearted prostitute who runs the Deadwood Saloon is, beneath her shabby calling, so goodhearted that she seems little short of saintly.

Japan is the most brilliant custodian of her own past. This makes sense, for today's Tokyo looks like today's Chicago, its people wear suits of Yankee cut, and the MacArthur dynasty has left its impress on the nation far more than the dynasty of Hirohito. The present is drab, the past ornate. Hence the movies which Japan sends to the outside world reconstruct the feudal age—a time of proud barons, pretty princesses and a Samurai code that enabled brave men to win honor with the sword. They are movies that indulge the exotic and our craving for fairy tales.

This age has vanished, of course, and yet in a way it represents the most enduring Japan of all—the world that is preserved in Japanese art. What bewitches us in a Japanese screen or print is its unerring color and design. When movies came along the Japanese used the medium with the same fastidious eye, and so their best films are like a classical print come to life. "Gate of Hell" was literally breathtaking from beginning to end. Many people remember it as their most vivid impression of Japan. It didn't represent the country as it is today. But it did represent the Japanese nature.

In the case of the United States the problem is peculiarly thorny. There is no corner of the globe that Hollywood's charades do not reach. In fact, now that the movie audience in this country is dwindling, our industry earns well over half of its money from foreign box-offices. Obviously the world's image of us is shaped almost entirely by our movies, and as many commentators have pointed out, this is not our best image, or even a fair one. We continue to breed clichés about our country that are just as rigid and false as the French cliché of the philandering mate or the British cliché of the funny bank robber.

What do we know of the Midwest through our movies? Very little. Not until "Picnic" in 1956 did I see a movie that captured the feeling of the farm belt. Joshua Logan made the film in a Kansas town so plain that it looked like a thousand other American towns. He photographed its homely frame houses with their porch swings, cluttered parlors and crab grass lawns that creep out over the sidewalk. He shot the brick high school and the sluggish river in the middle of town and the freight yards at the edge. Beyond the town he framed huge grain elevators against a pale blue sky and a flat landscape of wheat that stretched out to the horizon. He even recorded the sounds of summer, like the banging of the back screen door.

Thus he told the moviegoer that a small Midwest town is a tiny unit in the middle of nothing, that its interests are indrawn and its currents of gossip strong, and that those who break away to the outside world do so only by breaking off their entire past. This is a central fact of life in the Midwest—it affects those who stay as much as those who go—and it is a deeply dramatic fact. It is a theme dear to American literature, but "Picnic" marked its rare treatment on the screen. As the movie reached its climax at a Labor Day picnic—a supremely American event with its wheezy musicians on a flag-draped bandstand, its male quartets and shrill sopranos, its pie-eating contests, three-legged races, watermelons and lost babies—various characters also reached a turning point in their lives, and by then we were in a position to understand the factors of environment that shaped their decisions.

Here is an American vein that Hollywood has hardly tapped. Nor do I know much, as a movie fan, about the Southwest and Northwest—"Giant" and "Bus Stop" were only a beginning—and I know almost nothing about the booming state of California. And what about Hollywood's version of the South? The pre-Civil War days fall into a picturesque pattern long fixed by national folklore. Kindly old Massa rules the plantation not with a whip but a swizzle stick, while white-bewhiskered Negroes bring him juleps and sing spirituals in the cotton fields, as their mammies did before them, and Miss Eulabelle holds court to the local fops. This kind of thing is by now as stylized as the western.

But the modern South is a different matter. Its most celebrated bards are William Faulkner, Erskine Caldwell and Tennessee Williams, and from the movies based on their works we would assume the South to be inhabited solely by lynchers, barn burners, rapists, hillbillies, sex-starved blondes, vengeful old patriarchs and idiot sons. These pictures barely touched the human issues that make the South today one of America's most dramatic regions. It is an area afflicted by hatreds so old and inbred that they can be exorcised only in pain, an area where the bigots are far outnumbered by gentle citizens who sincerely want to solve the problem that darkens their lives. In this situation there are dozens of movies that would touch the heart.

Sometimes a good portrait of America comes from a surprising origin. Who would have thought that "Peyton Place" would be such a film? As everybody knows, the novel had little patience with its characters once they were out of bed and dressed, but it did have a New England setting, and from this threshold Hollywood made a movie that had an authentic American flavor.

Several of its plots were quite racy, but in general it dealt with the ordinary things that happen to people during the cycle of a New England year. First of all, it had pictorial beauty. Director Mark Robson realized that the town itself was one of the movie's stars, and he let his camera wander over its features—old white churches and elm-lined streets, clapboard houses and brick mills—so that, as the seasons changed from snow to drowsy summer and garish fall, the moviegoer had a feeling for the rhythm of the community. Against this background Robson shot some of the rituals that are part of the growing-up process in towns all over America. The movie also recognized that life has subtle seasons of its own, such as the summer after high school graduation, a summer that is like no other, bridging the world of child and adult. In these details "Peyton Place" touched some of America's deepest roots, for it sought plain truths and was satisfied to set them down plainly.

New York has been the subject of many movies, most of them swollen far beyond reality. They paint New Yorkers as a suave and wealthy breed, oscillating between penthouse and Stork Club, their girls a race of goddesses swathed in money and mink. It is a temptation hard to resist, for Manhattan has glamour, and if there's one thing that Hollywood wants to put on the screen it's glamour. That's what movies are for—to some extent. But recently quite a few films have also dealt with the real New Yorkers, the millions who do not have wealth or beauty or glamour, who are acutely lonely though they dwell in the most populous city on earth.

"Marty," of course, is the classic example of the movie that glimpsed the heartache of urban man. Tenderly and with humor it told the story of a pudgy Bronx butcher and a shy girl who had given up hope that love would ever find them. The movie looked real because it was filmed against real neon store fronts, subway stations and other such local landmarks. But that was not the secret of its spell. Its truth lay in the honesty of its dialogue and the purity of its vision, for never once did it make its characters do something unnatural for the sake of dramatic effect or cheapen their affair with a joke that didn't belong. Their search for love, and their wonder at discovering it, were touching because in this search everyone in the audience saw something of himself.

It was followed by quite a few other New York movies that had the same honesty, such as "A Hatful of Rain" and "Sweet Smell of Success," but these films were somewhat unsavory and they brought into the open a problem that has long vexed Americans who fear for our reputation. "Blackboard Jungle"—to take the most notorious—was a taut drama of violence in a New York high school, partly touched off by racial tensions. It did not reflect all American high schools and actually damaged our good name abroad.

Still, no believer in the American freedoms would say that the movie should not have been made, or that the government should forbid its sale outside this country. Censorship is the death of art. Nor can any censor foresee exactly what impression a movie will make, as "The Grapes of Wrath" once proved to the Kremlin's surprise. The Russians exhibited the picture widely, intending to illustrate the sordid nature of life in the United States. But the fact that the Okies had a car, decrepit as it was, put them one up on the Soviet moviegoers, and the film was withdrawn.

Hollywood is under no obligation to paint America in rosy colors. But the industry is financially obliged to save its skin, and all the tricks that science can devise—wide screens and stereophonic sound—will not bring Americans back into the movie house if the story is bad. There is a basic instinct about this. It is no accident that "Our Town"

is America's most durable drama. Year after year Thornton
Wilder's play is performed in hundreds of schools, colleges
and theatrical societies. It speaks to young and old, rich
and poor. It touches every man's experience because it deals
in universal truths.

Such stories abound in our land and Hollywood has not
begun to tell them. Every town in America is "Our Town"
if the moviemakers approach it from the right direction—
and know what to do when they get there.

17. Harold Arlen:

America's Secret Songwriter

WHEN THE TOURING "PORGY AND BESS" company visited Cairo nine years ago, some of its members went one afternoon to a local symphony concert. Most of the program was devoted to Mozart, Beethoven and other classical composers, and it ended with a section called "American Folk Music." This turned out to be a suite built around "Stormy Weather" and incorporating four other songs: "Blues in the Night," "I've Got a Right to Sing the Blues," "Accentuate the Positive" and "Ill Wind."

The American listeners were astonished, not only because the songs were all modern, but because they were all by the same man—Harold Arlen. After the concert Robert Breen, director of "Porgy and Bess," asked the Egyptian conductor if he knew who wrote the songs.

"But, sir," the conductor said, "nobody wrote them. They are just old American ballads that we made into a folk medley."

Breen looked at the printed music and saw a tiny pencil scrawl on one page that said H. ARLENE. "When I told the conductor that 'H. Arlene' was still alive," Breen recalls, "he just couldn't believe it."

The story confirms a feeling about Harold Arlen's music that is held in many parts of the world. In Europe his songs are heard everywhere, and quite a few are regarded as indigenous ballads dating from Stephen Foster's day. Yet nobody in Europe knows Arlen's name, and hardly anybody does in America, though addicts of his music here are legion. I have been one of these addicts since the early 1930's when I first heard "Stormy Weather" and "Ill Wind."

Like the Egyptian folklorist many years later, I was moved by something mysterious in these songs. Both of them had a plaintive melody and an insinuating rhythm that seemed peculiarly American and very old, as if they were Negro laments that originated in the South many generations ago. I was surprised to learn instead that they were newly written by Mr. Arlen (whom I had never heard of) for "The Cotton Club Revue," a semiannual Harlem revue that invoked the talents of Bill Robinson, Cab Calloway, Duke Ellington, Ethel Waters, Lena Horne and many other Negro stars, some already risen high, some barely ascendant.

Obviously Arlen had an uncanny instinct for the Negro idiom, in which sadness of melody coexists with jauntiness of beat. I sensed this not only in his music but in his voice, for several records were issued at the time on which Arlen sang "Stormy Weather" and some other Cotton Club songs. I remember the voice because it was so unusual—high as a schoolboy's, but emotional far beyond a schoolboy's years, and it had a pervading melancholy. I learned that he was not a Negro, but a Buffalo cantor's son in his late twenties. He was still in them when he moved in 1934 to Hollywood, where he settled down for a long spell of writing movie songs so superior that they took on a life of their own.

"Blues in the Night," for instance, is hummed the world over; the film of the same title was forgotten before its customers got out of the theater, and some couldn't get out fast enough. "That Old Black Magic" is a song of amazing durability. So are "Let's Fall in Love," "It's Only a Paper Moon," "One for My Baby and One More for the Road," "Accentuate the Positive," "Happiness Is Just a Thing Called Joe," "My Shining Hour" and "The Man That Got Away," though the movies that they embellished —like "Star-Spangled Rhythm" and "Here Come the Waves"—were no great shakes, if any shakes at all.

Only "The Wizard of Oz" matched as a film the standard of Arlen and his lyricist, E. Y. Harburg, whose score included one of the most popular of all American songs, "Over the Rainbow." It was the song, of course, that launched the very young Judy Garland, and ever since that wistful start Miss Garland has sung a high proportion of Arlen songs in her concerts and on her records.

In 1944 Arlen began writing for the theater again and composed such scores as "Bloomer Girl," "St. Louis Woman," "House of Flowers," "Jamaica," "Saratoga" and "Blue Opera," the latter given a brief tryout in Europe but still unproduced here. Through each of these scores ran certain songs so original in melody and distinctive in harmonic structure that, while no two were alike, the stamp of their composer—a deep loneliness—was on them all. "Come Rain or Come Shine," "I Wonder What Became of Me" and "Sleepin' Bee," three of Arlen's finest ballads, are examples.

As most of these late numbers were written for Negroes, they seemed an extension, now far more mature, of the idiom that Arlen had caught so intuitively in his Cotton Club days. They also seemed an extension of the idiom that George Gershwin captured in his Negro folk opera, "Porgy and Bess." Arlen is Gershwin's closest heir in his blue melodic and harmonic line. Sometimes, in fact, Gershwin came close to Arlen, as in "Bess, You Is My Woman Now," whose opening curve is akin to that of "Ill Wind." Gershwin didn't have to borrow from anybody, nor does Arlen, but the two men admired each other's work and had kindred backgrounds, so it is no accident that their songs have the same American restlessness, while most of our other great theater composers—notably Jerome Kern, Richard Rodgers and Frank Loesser—are nearer in their lilting airs to the traditions of European light opera.

It is this Americanism that makes Gershwin's "Porgy and Bess" so contagious. It has smitten audiences equally in Yugoslavia and Japan, Germany and Brazil. In its score people everywhere seem to find the traits that give America her personality—not only brittle rhythms and captivating melodies, but excitement and humor and truth. These qualities are also in Arlen's songs. Where did they come from—and why should these two men write music so congenial to Negroes?

Harold Arlen, who is now sixty and lives in New York, is a slender man with short black hair and deep blue eyes, whose face would be his fortune if his songs were not. At least it is the kind that painters and photographers prize, for it has much in common with that favorite subject of theirs, the tragic clown. It is a vertical face, properly belonging to a blues writer, and in repose it has a loneliness that appears to have been fashioned by decades of sorrow, if not generations. Much of this is inborn; much has been imprinted by real travails in Arlen's life, including an illness a decade ago that he narrowly survived, and the rest is simply the emotional residue left on the composer by the act of composing, for in this process he is a man totally engaged.

But the most arresting qualities about Arlen are gentleness and generosity. He is shy about discussing his music and uneasy with praise. Though his features relax naturally into dolor, they brighten quickly whenever something funny is said, and frequently he is the one who says it. Any fan would guess this about Arlen, for there is a current of humor that runs through many of his songs and gives them vitality. In "We're Off to See the Wizard," "Evelina," "A Woman's Prerogative" and "Let's Take a Walk Around the Block"—to choose four at random from different phases of his career—a genial lyrical idea is set to a tune that bubbles with enjoyment, or, as in "Accentuate the Positive," to a delayed syncopation that gives the words an extra antic value.

Arlen has no trouble tracing his musical gift. "My father was the best of the cantors," he says, his voice rustier now than the one I had heard on records long ago, but still a rare instrument. "All the cantors came to my father's synagogue in Buffalo while I was growing up, but he was the best. He improvised wonderful melodies to fit the texts that had no music, and that's undoubtedly where my sense of melody comes from.

"I learned to play the piano and sing. My big interest

was in the jazz instrumentalists of the day. I even ran
away from home once to hear the Memphis Five, a Dixie-
land group. They were my heroes. At fifteen I quit school
and formed 'The Snappy Trio.' We played in night clubs
around town and eventually grew into a quintet called
'The Southbound Shufflers,' working mostly on the lake
steamers out of Buffalo. In time we grew into an eleven-
man band called 'The Buffalodians.' " He smiled at the
remote and corny names, so redolent of the Prohibition
era in American jazz. "I was the singer, pianist and
arranger. I could always improvise, and I loved to invent
unconventional turns for the men in the band who
couldn't do anything but follow the written melody. I
wanted them to get off it and sound like somebody from
New York."

Even better than to be in Buffalo and sound like somebody in New York, of course, was to be in the big city
itself, and Arlen migrated there at twenty-two. He served
in his triple capacity for various bands, the most famous
being that of Arnold Johnson, and still considered himself a vocalist above all. He had never thought of writing
songs.

This change of direction came about by accident in 1929
during rehearsals of Vincent Youmans' "Great Day," for
which he had been hired as a singer. When the rehearsal
pianist became ill, Arlen filled in briefly, and in impro-
vising a "vamp" for the dancers he came up with something so catchy that it caught everyone within earshot.
Admirers of the tune introduced Arlen to Ted Koehler,
who set a lyric to it, and the resulting number was sung
by Ruth Etting as the finale of the "9:15 Revue" the
following season. It was his first hit: "Get Happy."

Thus Koehler became the earliest of the gifted lyricists
who have worked with Arlen, and the boy from Buffalo

was lucky to find him at this pivotal moment. Koehler had rhythm and an ear for the colloquial, judging not only by "Stormy Weather," whose lyric is as much a classic as its melody, but by the many other infectious songs that he and Arlen wrote between 1930 and 1934 for eight Cotton Club revues, such as "I've Got the World on a String" and "Between the Devil and the Deep Blue Sea."

To what extent Arlen was consciously writing for Negroes in these shows is something that even he can't remember, though he does recall that he wrote "Stormy Weather" for Cab Calloway, the first three notes being conceived as a springboard for one of Calloway's "shouts." But Cab never got to sing it. Arlen himself made a recording of the song that swept the country before the Cotton Club revue of 1933 opened, and the producers, realizing they had a torch song of considerable value on their hands, brought Ethel Waters out of retirement for the occasion. People flocked to the show mainly to hear the song, and Miss Waters was identified with it for many years.

"Blues in the Night" was born in a somewhat similar manner. Arlen and Johnny Mercer were commissioned in 1941 to write the score for a movie that was to be a serious study of an American jazz band, and to include in it one hit song of a blues nature.

"I went home and just thought about it for two days," Arlen recalls. "After all, anybody can write a blues song. The hard thing is to write one that doesn't sound like every other blues song. Finally I decided to cast it in the traditional form of the early American blues—that is, three sections of twelve bars each, rather than in the conventional Tin Pan Alley shape," which is, of course, thirty-two bars of a-a-b-a or a-b-a-b. He met his own challenge by writing three memorable themes, rounding off the song with a repeat of the first twelve bars and a four-bar coda, so that the total number came to fifty-two, or twenty more than the rules allow.

Mercer remembers that it was a hard lyric to write because of its meandering length, but he resisted official attempts to eliminate the song's third section, thereby saving one of Arlen's most haunting melodies. And Arlen remembers plucking the words "My mama done tole me" from the bottom of the lyric to the top, where "From Natchez to Mobile" had originally stood, thereby giving world currency to that newly minted idiom. The whole lyric, in fact, is so right, catching the loneliness of the music in images like that of the echoing train whistle and the responsive mockingbird ("take my word, the mockingbird will sing the saddest kind of song, he knows things are wrong"), that it stirs fresh admiration still.

When "Blues in the Night" was completed, Arlen went over to Jerome Kern's house and played it for him. Kern listened and then, Arlen says, "went away and came back with Offenbach's ivory-handled cane, which Alexander Woollcott had given him, and presented it to me." Arlen, while he regarded the gift as a sign that he had written a good song, nevertheless found it enigmatic, seeing no lineal descent between "Tales of Hoffmann" and his own forlorn ballad. But Kern had his reasons, and they can be found in the encyclopedia, which says that "Jacques Levy Offenbach, 1819-80, French composer, was the son of a Jewish cantor." Obviously the cane has found its proper owner in the twentieth century. Where Woollcott got it Arlen can't imagine, and who could?

The first recordings were such an overnight hit that Warner Brothers hurriedly changed their movie's title to "Blues in the Night," hoping to salvage with fifty-two bars of music the atrocity which they had by then committed in two hours of film. But honor was beyond saving, except possibly for Elia Kazan, who played the clarinet in a small role, and of course for Arlen and Mercer, whose score also contained the lovely ballad "This Time the Dream's on Me."

Mercer, who is from Savannah, sees Arlen's work as a fusion of classical Jewish music with early Negro jazz—a combination that keeps the lyricist alert for anything. "Harold's melodies are way out because Jewish melodies are way out—they take unexpected twists and turns," Mercer says, thus defining the term "way out" as well as Arlen's songs. Mercer might have been thinking of the fact that "Come Rain or Come Shine" begins in one key and ends in another, or of the odd pattern of "That Old Black Magic," which runs to seventy-two bars, never exactly repeating what has gone before but always developing the earlier material logically.

To Mercer there is a strong affinity between Gershwin and Arlen, especially in their grasp of Negro idioms, and he thinks that this stems largely from the kind of music that they listened to in their youth. "When George and Harold were little boys, growing up within about five years of each other," he points out, "they were hearing records of Negro spirituals like 'Swing Low' and 'Motherless Chile,' and they were also hearing the very early jazz recordings of men like King Oliver. They couldn't help being influenced, just as Irving Berlin, for instance, was influenced in 'Alexander's Ragtime Band' by the still earlier minstrel shows and street parades.

"Arlen is more inventive than Gershwin in trying to find new forms for his songs. The rhythm of both men is wonderful, but George's often strikes me as mathematical —listen to the precision of 'Sweet and Low Down' or 'Fascinatin'· Rhythm'—while Harold's comes from the bottom of his feet."

Ira Gershwin, who has collaborated with Arlen on such

old Broadway scores as "Life Begins at 8:40" and such
recent movie scores as "A Star Is Born," agrees that Arlen
in his blue vein is an extension of George Gershwin in
his. "But Harold is no imitator," he says. "He is always
original, always himself. His songs are, well, *peculiarly*
constructed, so that I never know what to expect. I remember thinking that 'The Man That Got Away' was too
long and unorthodox to be a hit, but it grew on people.
Harold's songs always do.

"To me the Hebraic influence is the big one in his
music, and it's something that my brother George didn't
have. Our parents, like Harold's, came from Eastern Rus-
sia, but there was no Jewish religious music in our family
—in fact, no music at all until one day, when George was
about eleven, we got a piano and he sat down and played
some songs with all the right chords."

If Gershwin's "Porgy and Bess," with its nervous rhythms
and searching melodies, seems to contain Negro folk elements, as Arlen's "Blues Opera" does, that may be because
of a subtle emotional tie between the two races. Certainly
a Jewish composer, conscious of the uprooted history of
his people, would be attuned to the similar plight of the
American Negro. Arlen, who believes in such mystical
forces in music, has a mystical hunch that this is so.

Arlen has worked with only one lyricist who was a
stranger to the musical theater, Truman Capote. The show
that they wrote together, "House of Flowers," though im-
perfect, was touched with freshness and beauty. With
Capote, Arlen achieved certain effects more sensitive than
anything he had done before, such as the superb song,
"I Never Has Seen Snow." Yet their collaboration began
under conditions that were hardly ideal.

"We worked together the first three months without

personal contact," Capote recalls. During this time I was living in Rome, while his base was California. I would send him scenes and scraps of lyrics, and back came homemade phonograph records: Arlen playing melodies that the tentative lyrics had tentatively suggested, singing and talking to me. We had never met, I knew very little about him. It was quite odd, listening to this disembodied voice and trying to derive from it some notion of what sort of man he might be, my collaborator. Obviously he was a gentle man, a modest one, but someone capable of immense intensity; and, had I not known differently, I would have thought he was a Negro. His voice, especially his singing voice, had a warm, plaintive, muddy-colored tone, and the diction also had a certain very pleasant Negro quality.

"Eventually, when I did meet Arlen and we began to work together, I found all my long-distance impressions confirmed. The sadness, the echo of loneliness that wails through much of Arlen's music, seemed to me the foundation of his sensibility, for he is a man obsessed by the tragic view of life. At the same time, amid the sighs, the long sad looks, laughter was always ready to run rampant. He has one of the most distinctive laughs I've ever heard —a wild, high-pitched chuckling that reddens his face and fills his eyes with tears.

"I had no true understanding of song writing (and Lord knows, still do not). But Arlen, who I suppose had never worked with an amateur before, was tolerant and infinitely encouraging and, well, just a gent about the whole thing. A brave gent, too. Twice he spent long and seriously ill spells in the hospital where, against doctors' orders, against all the laws of human fortitude as well, he continued composing. It was one rainy winter afternoon, while he was hospitalized, that we made up 'Two Ladies in de Shade

of de Banana Tree'—Arlen, weak and ghost-pale, tapping
out the rhythm with a pencil and humming at, very literally, death's door.

"For him, music is the entire story. There, inside a
world of sound, he is always courageous, intelligent, in-
capable of cliché. His songs almost invariably contain some
melodic surprise, some *difficulty*—which is one of the
reasons he has not had the recognition he deserves. He is
too versatile and inventive to have created a large single
image, an Arlen *sound,* in the sense that Porter and Gershwin have a sound. Of course, for those who really know
his music, Arlen has a sound, a style, that is immediately
recognizable, one more haunting and original than any
of his contemporaries: a real blues in the night."

If Arlen's various lyric writers have been one cause of
his anonymity, they have also stretched him in new directions. To each man's lyrics he responds differently, which
is an index of his fertile imagination.

His most frequent lyricist, over twenty-five years, has
been E. Y. ("Yip") Harburg. Harburg, who has written
with other composers such fine songs as "April in Paris"
and such scores as "Finian's Rainbow," strives for the
poetic image in his lyrics. Consequently he touches off in
Arlen a quality that is almost stately, as in "Last Night
When We Were Young" (Arlen's own favorite) or "Right
As the Rain." Though these songs are a different facet
of their composer, they are as typical of him as the humorous melodies that he often writes with Mercer, such as
"Hit the Road to Dreamland." They are the results of a
relentless effort not to be typed.

"But," Arlen says with a wan smile, as if doing obei-
sance to the joke that fate has played him, "I'm typed as
a blues writer and there's nothing I can do about it. What's
blue about 'My Shining Hour,' or 'Let's Take the Long

Way Home,' or—well, I could name many." He could, too, and that's what makes the joke so wry. "My Shining Hour," for instance, is such a pure and soaring tune that you might think Jerome Kern had written it.

If Arlen started to name his gay songs, he could include the entire score of "Bloomer Girl." This Broadway hit of 1944 was a singularly sunny piece of work. To Harburg's lyrics Arlen wrote fourteen blithe and graceful numbers, including three waltzes, that have an attractive unity and seem true to their Civil War period. Only in one other case did Arlen create such a joyful unit, and that was in "The Wizard of Oz." There he and Harburg succeeded remarkably in entering the world of children. Though there are few surer ways of making enemies than to dramatize a childhood classic, only the most churlish devotee of Frank Baum's fantasy land would deny that this film caught the spirit of, as one of the songs was titled, "the merry old land of Oz."

Of course the actors, especially Ray Bolger as the scarecrow and Bert Lahr as the fainthearted lion, were accountable for much of the movie's spell, but it was the score that set and sustained the mood. Even so, M-G-M had its worries. "This score is above the heads of children," one executive told Harburg. He was wrong, needless to say, though it is true that the music and lyrics are more sophisticated than they seem. "If I Only Had a Heart," for example, is no simple nursery rhyme.

At any rate, Arlen and Harburg had the satisfaction of appealing to children without talking down to them. Ironically, they met the stiffest studio resistance in the case of "Over the Rainbow," which M-G-M removed three times during the picture's production. Finally saved from the cutting-room floor, the song won the Academy Award and began a career that will be hard to match for longevity.

Longevity is, in Harburg's opinion, one of the three keys to Arlen's genius. "His songs get better with time," he says. "You don't tire of them, as you do with most pop tunes. Often they're not easy to get at first—the public has to grow up to understand them. But if you have faith in what you're doing, as Harold has, you don't worry about that." (The chances of Arlen's not worrying are small, but he frets less than he once did over the fact that his songs frequently are slow starters. Quite a few, like "Happiness Is Just a Thing Called Joe," didn't catch on literally for years.)

The second attribute of Arlen's music, Harburg feels, is its universal appeal. "A lot of people can write songs," he says, "but only an artist can make other people feel the music deeply. Harold touches something in all of us that responds. But what he has above all is individuality. He and George Gershwin are the two men in our field who uniquely have this gift—they make a contribution, break ground, do something that hasn't been done before."

Like Mercer, Ira Gershwin and Capote—in fact, in almost the same words—Harburg cited the knotty problems that Arlen hands his lyric writers. "He leads you into situations that are unanticipated," Harburg says. "I often have to wait a day or two to let the melody work on me, to see what Harold is really doing. And he's so afraid of being banal that he revises over and over." All of Arlen's collaborators, incidentally, share an affection for the man that matches their admiration for his music.

To his fans Arlen's masterpiece is a Negro musical of 1946 called "St. Louis Woman," whose lyrics are also Mercer's masterpiece. In this show, based on a book by the Negro writers Arna Bontemps and Countee Cullen, Arlen's instincts for Negro folk opera blossomed luxuriantly. The score was all that an old fan could have hoped for. It had humorous songs and rhythm songs, blues to break the heart, such as "I Had Myself a True Love," and cakewalks and chorales and lullabies. It was all of a piece, and it was exciting and good.

Despite my repeated attendance in the second balcony, the show folded after 131 performances, and one of Broadways finest scores seemed lost forever. But in 1954 Robert Breen commissioned Arlen to write an opera around "St. Louis Woman," and so "Blues Opera" was born. Using as a foundation the original twelve songs and several of his older laments like "Blues in the Night," Arlen spent the next few years composing a full-length score.

The new material is even more exhilarating than what was already there. It consists of dialogue set to music, but instead of emerging as recitative, it has spilled out in a variety of forms that are unfailingly melodic and often breathtaking in rhythm, even if they are nothing more than fragments, or exhortations at the racetrack and gambling table, or street hawkers' calls. Sometimes they fall, perhaps only subconsciously, into traditional Negro forms— into spirituals, for instance, that sound plantation-born.

I listened to the score on a makeshift tape recording. Arlen himself was playing the piano and singing most of the parts. A generation had passed since I first heard that sensuous voice and the grieving strains of "Stormy Weather," both of which augured so much. Now the voice was unburdening itself of some of the richest "Negro" music—and richest Arlen music—that I had ever heard. This, needless to say, was Nirvana. For though across the years I had also been collecting Gershwin, Rodgers, Porter, Kern and other great "show tune" composers, Arlen was my secret vice—secret, among other reasons, because Arlen himself is one of our national secrets, a man as unsung as his music is not.

18. *The Vanishing Boffola*

Of all the ancient monuments in London none impressed me so much for sheer durability, not even Westminster Abbey, as a sextet of vaudeville comics known collectively as "The Crazy Gang." The fact that their individual names twice contain "&"—they are Nervo & Knox, Bud Flanagan, Naughton & Gold, and "Monsewer" Eddie Gray—suggests that they are an agglomeration of old variety acts, as indeed they have been for thirty years, and the fact that one of them bears the cognomen "Monsewer" is a fair index to their group taste in humor.

They are said to be the favorite entertainers of the Royal Family, which doesn't bode too well for the monarchy, if true—and it probably is, for when I saw their revue, "Clown Jewels," a photograph of Queen Elizabeth smiled ecstatically down on her subjects from a wall in the theater lobby. And yet I think I understand, if a mere commoner may make such surmises, what it is about the six buffoons that the Queen finds so diverting.

At the time of my visit, "Clown Jewels" had been running, at two shows nightly, for 600 performances, and I expected lines of fatigue to be etched deeply on its corporate brow. Friends had warned me that a few pre-theater drinks would make the evening bearable, if not necessarily enjoyable, and though I took the precaution of following their advice, bourbon was only half responsible for the glow of anticipation with which I settled into my seat. I was also making a pilgrimage to the memory of my last trip to London.

That had been in 1939, when as an adolescent I was taken by my father to the Palladium. So funny were its comedians, so hilarious its acts, that the word "Palladium" fixed itself in my lexicon as a synonym for paradise, and when I returned to London I lost no time looking in the papers to see what was playing there.

What was playing there was Liberace, who occupies quite a different corner of my lexicon. On asking what had become of vaudeville, I learned that it has almost completely vanished from England and that the hallowed Palladium is now inhabited by ordinary mortals—crooners, drummers and such. So I went in desperation to the Crazy Gang, hoping to find in them some flickering spark of the enchanted past.

In appearance, at least, they fitted the classic image. Four of them reminded me, by a pleasant coincidence, of the great Bert Lahr, Bobby Clark, Victor Moore and Groucho Marx, The other two reminded me of Olsen & Johnson, and as it soon turned out, the spiritual kinship of all six was closest to those two knockabouts, who shepherded "Hellzapoppin'" across America for what seemed like a solid decade, if not eternity.

Old age had overtaken them. Flanagan, who appeared before one backdrop that said "Born 1896 and Still Going Wrong," was probably the youngest. The others had reached that autumnal stage where potbellies rest ludicrously on skinny white legs—a condition not noticeable in most trades that old men practice, but hard to conceal in clowns who frequently lose their trousers or dress up as girls.

Both these routines were staples of the Crazy Gang's repertory. At one point they turned up as debutantes being presented at Buckingham Palace and looking quite grotesque—especially one dotard who was well into his seventies and who, we were informed, had just been married. His probable debility as a bridegroom lent itself to four or five jokes, none of them subtle (several were built on allusions to the Battersea power plant); for the Crazy Gang were not strict believers in the purity of the spoken word.

And yet there was a certain innocence about their show, not only in its skits but in its production numbers. At one point Flanagan sang a ballad called "Strollin'," which, though new, had the period flavor of "In the Good Old Summertime" or "Bicycle Built for Two." It extolled the pleasures of a moonlight stroll, whereupon the curtains parted and the entire chorus—girls with parasols and boys in boaters—ambled arm in arm across the darkened stage, singing. It was so naïve and unabashed that it was irresistible.

Many other numbers were similar throwbacks to early forms of mummery. Quite late in the evening "Monsewer"

Eddie Gray, who had figured in various wheezy skits up to that moment, came on alone and revealed his true origins in show business. He manipulated a half-dozen large hoops with such consummate skill that I could have watched him all night. He was, in his own field, a great artist—the kind that used to comprise a whole night's bill in London's Palladium and New York's Palace, and whose disappearance has left vast multitudes with nothing but their memories and a vague, pathetic craving.

Less refined, but equally basic in appeal, was a scene near the end of "Clown Jewels" in which two Crazy Gangers, sitting in one of those mezzanine boxes that overhang the stage, threw oranges at their colleagues below, pelting them when their backs were turned and sometimes, with surprising accuracy, knocking their hats off. Between throws they all exchanged a great deal of banter which, by any standards of humor, was a long way from being good. But the two comedians in the box were so convulsed by what they were saying and doing (though they had done it earlier that very night and 600-odd times before) that they could hardly speak their lines, and again I was swept along in the contagion of the event.

For one thing, I am a sucker for the simple humor of the flying object, or even the wielded object. Let one baggy-pants clown hit another with a bladder, for instance, and I will be in a seizure of joy. But what really delighted me about the scene, and about "Clown Jewels" as a whole, was that its six old men were so endearingly eager to please the audience and so easily pleased themselves. Whatever burlesque talents they may once have had were now rusted over, and their voices were almost as scratchy as their jokes. But they had never lost, in the hundreds of years and countless thousands of nights that their careers encompassed, their fresh enthusiasm for comedy's oldest tools.

The fact that they used these tools poorly didn't bother

me. I laughed throughout, at times uncontrollably, and so did the capacity audience. I laughed partly because some gags were funny, and partly because some were so terrible, but mostly because I was having a good time. I was being offered pure entertainment—a commodity that an American can hardly get in his own country any more, unless Danny Kaye is at large or unless he has access to the silent films of Mack Sennett, Buster Keaton, Laurel & Hardy and other masters of the visual joke.

For humor has largely gone out of our arts, and where it does survive it is seldom humor for its own sake. The nation now takes itself so seriously that even its jokes must have a point, and our most honored wits are those like Mort Sahl, or Mike Nichols and Elaine May, whose sallies are edged with meaning. They should, of course, be honored—they are brilliant, and we need them. If their humor is somewhat "sick," these are sick times, and perhaps only our satirists and parodists can help us see the malaise and cure it. But when we laugh at comics like Sahl we are working hard. They require of us a mental effort and a taste for irony.

There remains the problem, also important to a country's health, of making people laugh spontaneously, and the practitioners of this art are nearly extinct. Chaplin has turned into other paths. The Marx Brothers have closed up shop. W. C. Fields and Bobby Clark are dead. Bert Lahr and Nancy Walker languish for lack of material. Sid Caesar has the instincts, and so does Donald O'Connor, but they are seldom employed, for humor is a commercial risk in this land of the renowned sense of humor.

Fun and farce have been gone from Broadway for many seasons—the theater is in a gloomy and introverted mood. Broadway could use, heretical as this may seem in the era of "integrated" musicals, a few grab-bag shows—like

George White's "Scandals" or Ziegfeld's "Follies"—whose aim is simply to amuse the audience and whose songs do not advance the plot because there is no plot to advance. "A Funny Thing Happened on the Way to the Forum" is a good start back in that direction.

Funny movies come along once a year, if we are lucky, and we are pitifully thankful to the men who create them. Billy Wilder, probably Hollywood's wittiest craftsman, basked in the gratitude of the populace—and in huge profits—for writing and directing "Some Like It Hot." Its mere presence in the movie houses of America brought pleasant echoes of the years when Hollywood gave us a steady diet of comedies, like "It Happened One Night," "The Thin Man," "The Great McGinty" and—well, anybody over thirty can name dozens. But Wilder is also a moralist, and his next film, "The Apartment," though frequently droll, had such sardonic overtones that a moviegoer didn't really know whether to laugh or cry. Thus even our movie comedies have lost their essential gaiety. "Dr. Strangelove, or How I Learned to Stop Worrying and Love the Bomb," probably the funniest of recent American movies, is also one of the most serious morality tales that the nation has ever been served.

It is time for the boff and the belly laugh to be heard in the land again. Let bladders resound and prats fall, let top bananas grow on trees. Let some poor pantaloon tumble into the bass drum or into a bin of flour. Let him even—I am this desperate—see pie in the sky, headed for him. Let some impresario mount a full evening of vaudeville, bringing "Monsewer" Eddie Gray and his hoops from London and leaving his jokes behind. If this be treason, I can always move to England. It's anything but *lèse-majesté* over there.

19. Confessions of a Celluloid Eater

I AM NO ORDINARY TELEVISION ADDICT. My fixation takes a very specialized form, seizing me by surprise as I sit before the TV set idly twisting the dials. All sorts of "live" and topical programs flash by—interviews, news events, discussion panels, musical revues, weather predictions—and I quickly switch to other stations.

Then, suddenly, there appears on the screen an image so gray and fuzzy that nobody is recognizable at first glance. A closer look reveals the man to be George Raft, the girl to be Constance Bennett, and the period to be 1935 or thereabouts. It is, in short, an old movie. My hand freezes on the dial and I go into a kind of trance. Usually the movie is quite a bad one—some charade that stirred waves of apathy even when it was new. This doesn't matter; I am its bonded slave.

My addiction has some of its roots, of course, in nostalgia. I grew up in the decade before World War II, when people went to "the movies" as a habit. The act of going to a picture had excitement. To see the theater from afar and glimpse the movie's title, compressed onto a marquee too small to hold its multiple wonders (MUTINY ON BOUNTY C. GABLE); to come near and meet the commingled smells of popcorn and early air-conditioning, and to watch the usher tear the ticket with a snap of his wrists —these symbolized a clean break with the world outside. Sure enough, there on the screen C. Gable was doing nothing less fantastic than putting C. (for Captain) Bligh overboard in a little boat.

When these vintage films turn up on TV, they can hardly help conjuring up memories. But they are more than just a sentimental exercise. They are also a museum of America's immediate past, of the years roughly from Repeal to Eisenhower, and anyone who watches them can play the various games that almost every museum offers—games of pure delight at the curious shape of yesterday's objects, games of wonder at the changes in taste that occur between one generation and another.

I remember the musicals of Fred Astaire and Ginger Rogers, for instance, as the apex of sophistication. Dialogue so witty and urbane, production numbers so spectacular, heroines as ravishing as Miss Rogers could not be expected to come along a second time in this century. They did. When "Top Hat" ran on television recently, I watched it as I might a costume ball. Miss Rogers capered through some dances which, like the script and her dresses, were charming antiques. As for her coiffure, once so perfect that I wouldn't have wanted to change a hair of it, I now wanted to leave no hair unchanged.

The shifting feminine hairdo is nowhere better catalogued than in old movies on TV. Even in everyday life it is a phenomenon that baffles the male—a woman who wants to hide from her husband need only visit her hairdresser—so it is no wonder that I fail to recognize in early films the starlets who were the apple of my adolescent eye. Their faces strike a faint echo, but did their hair always look so funny? The evidence is there.

What the evidence says is that our standards are never as absolute as we think. One year's chic dress is another's Mother Hubbard, and in the field of interior decoration almost every fancy is a passing fancy. I remember how "smart" the living rooms and bedrooms looked in the movies of my youth, with their modern furniture of bleached wood and tubular metal and their white telephones. Today these rooms, playing a return engagement on TV, look as old and foolish as a Turkish corner.

Of course it's possible that these "smart" movie rooms never really existed, but were simply Hollywood's idea of how a smart room ought to look. For Carole Lombard to sprawl across an enormous bed, its coverlet and headboard made of tufted white satin, and talk on a white telephone while seeing her reflection in mirrors on three walls, was the quintessence of glamour, and some decorators of the '30s undoubtedly copied the effect. But they copied it only up to a point. For they knew, just as we all secretly suspected, that these Hollywood rooms were ultra-chichi and would date rapidly (which they did).

Though the rooms were too flamboyant to be true, we all accepted the untruth gladly, just for the fun of it. After all, one of Hollywood's functions is to manufacture dreams.

To what extent Hollywood's dreams became the reality, in many areas of life, is something that the old-movie watcher can ponder.

Nor is it only in inanimate objects that the mode is soon outmoded. Faces also change, and in changing give the old movie addict another game to tide him over the plot's dry stretches, which are anything but few and far between. (They are near between.) It is a recognition game, and can only be played by someone who tunes in on a picture after it has begun and the cast has been announced.

An actor will loom onto the screen who looks vaguely familiar—a gangling boy, perhaps, with awkward manner and bushy hair. I identify him quickly and announce the incredible news: "Why that's Jimmy *Stewart!*" Sometimes the discovery is put in the form of a question: "Is that Gary *Cooper?*"

We speak these sentences in tones of disbelief because our fixed image of the star has been broken. Stewart is a middle-aged man with thinning gray hair, not that callow lad filibustering on the Senate floor in "Mr. Smith Goes to Washington." Cooper was a creased old cowpoke, not that lineless youth making love in "A Farewell to Arms" to Helen Hayes, and *she* is the kindly matriarch of Broadway.

It is an eerie business, this reversing of the calendar. Never before have entertainers been in the position of competing with their younger selves. In such a match, youth would seem to have a sure edge. But this isn't always the case. Though it is a canon of American life to equate beauty with youth, and much of our advertising is directed toward that end, the star grown older is often far handsomer than the star new-born.

Humphrey Bogart was a fascinating young punk in "The Petrified Forest" in 1936, but he was a much more fascinating hero in "Casablanca" in 1942, and by the time "The African Queen" came along a decade later he was little short of irresistible. Onto a tough and homely visage the years stamped charm and humor and even a certain good looks. This singular feat of nature can be observed by the movie addict, if he is lucky, within the space of a week or two on TV, and it is only one of many such progressions.

Robert Taylor was almost too beautiful in "Camille" with Greta Garbo. Time made a man of him. Tyrone Power in his early career was a fine broth of a boy, as his countrymen say, but fairly thin broth. Cary Grant was probably born debonair (as well as being born Archibald Leach), but was he not more debonair at fifty than at thirty?

Faces don't always improve with age. The history of Hollywood is full of butterflies who turned back into moths. The young Franchot Tone, for instance, defending the Empire on India's northwest frontier in "Lives of a Bengal Lancer," had a shiny innocence that gradually lost its burnish. John Wayne, who has been called the great stone face (though probably not to his stone face), did not begin to ossify until after "Stagecoach." Only Astaire has managed to keep time's winged chariot chained to the ground. In his early movies and his late movies he is the same man, equally engaging, equally infallible in his approach to dance, women and song.

As for the ladies, they also run the distance race with varying degrees of success. The nightly watcher of television knows all types. He sees the pretty girls who rose to one leading role amid paeans of press-agentry and then fell back into oblivion—blondes as indistinguishable as the Misses Rheingold. For them, maids who pursued and caught their dream but couldn't hold it, the TV gazer feels a fleeting pang of recognition and regret. They lacked one important quality.

What they lacked was individuality—some personal stamp, some special style that set them apart from all the other merely pretty girls. They were products of a society that cherished conformity—an urge stronger than ever today. The Hollywood actresses who last, like Katharine Hepburn, Joan Crawford, Marlene Dietrich and Bette Davis, are the ones who have unique markings and stand apart from the herd of matching blondes. The old-movie addict can trace the careers of these durable ladies for three decades on TV and catch a fourth decade at the local movie house, for they are still going strong.

There is another type of actress who reflects a particular period—one that either she or the country later outgrew. Deanna Durbin was one of these special phenomena. A child of fresh beauty and pure voice, she sang in one movie after another through the years of emerging girlhood, and when all traces of the child were finally gone, her movie career ended, as it should have, for she would never have been quite the same again. Sonja Henie was another such visiting meteor. Ice was her element, as music was Deanna Durbin's and anguish is Joan Crawford's, and she skated into America's hearts with such success that we seemed to have been waiting just for her since 1776.

Ladies of this type, frozen into one narrow moment of our entertainment history, are among my favorite museum trophies on TV. There are others, of course. Betty Grable, the shape that launched 1,500,000 pin-ups to servicemen during World War II, appears in retrospect to have been the most formidable weapon in the arsenal of democracy during those dark years. Alice Faye seems to belong peculiarly to a rusty form of musical co-starring Cesar Romero and Don Ameche, and Merle Oberon turns up so often in old movies—through what quirk of booking I can't imagine—as to give the impression that she was the reigning star of the 1930s, which she wasn't.

But of course there was never a phenomenon as phenomenal as Shirley Temple. For countless mothers now in their early thirties, there are few more emotional experiences on TV than to see these films again with their own children. Generally the mothers introduce their children to Shirley with some trepidation, fearful that she might be too simple and sunny for this overexposed generation, which swallows bloody westerns neat at the age of four. It is the same nervousness that attends giving a child the favorite book of one's youth, for the magic does not always carry from one generation to the next.

Luckily, in good children's books like "The Wizard of Oz," it does, and Shirley Temple's films have the same quality of a childhood classic. They are hopelessly dated— no child could conquer America today as Shirley did in the 1930s. Those naive movies which she made with such gratifying frequency, tales that enabled her to tap-dance and sing songs about good ships "Lollipop," to beguile adults with her smile and to sulk when things went wrong, are creatures of their decade as surely as "Little Women" is the creature of its Victorian era. Yet they are still appealing, still very good of their type. The little girl that Shirley was—and *how* little she was—continues to cast her spell over other little girls sitting before the TV set, proving to them that fairy tales do exist and that life is not all cowboys and Indians,

There are many other types of movies that are no longer being made in America. The old film addict sees them and suddenly thinks: "What ever became of that kind of picture?" Old "society" movies, for example, are quite common on TV. They take place in palatial homes and they involve a harrumphing father, haughty mother, debutante daughter, weak suitor and comic butler, the latter invariably being Arthur Treacher or Eric Blore.

Nowadays there are no such movies, mainly because there aren't many such households, or, if there are, they no longer strike us as unbearably droll. The only millionaire who is still regarded as fair game is the Texas oilman, and he is quite a different fish from the purebred gentleman of the old Eastern society movie. He is a rough diamond. He represents all of us—Everyman who made it to the top with a little bit of luck, a great deal of brass and an enormous amount of oil.

Another extinct movie is the college frolic. The old film fan comes across it often on TV, amazed to find that higher education used to revolve mainly around football coaches of the Jack Oakie variety. The cultural temples at dear old Tech were the stadium, the girls' dormitory and the snack lounge. Since World War II, education has become a serious pursuit, and any campus film today would have to forsake the gridiron and nose around the astrophysics lab and graduate school, where life would be less jolly.

Audiences accepted these empty plots with a tolerant smile in the years before Pearl Harbor. The fact that they won't accept them as eagerly today is one sign that the country is growing up. To watch this process, to see the fabric of American life changing perceptibly, like a flower blooming in a speeded-up motion picture, is one of the richest rewards open to the old-movie addict.

Almost as obsolete as the society and college movie is the funny movie. Luckily, it survives on television. The old comedies like "My Favorite Wife" and "The Awful Truth," most of which seemed to star Cary Grant and Irene Dunne, may not be as antic now as they once were, but at least the people who made them were *trying* to be funny, and that type is hardly around any more. As a matter of fact, certain comedies are available on TV which will never be out-dated, or outdone. One, W. C. Fields's "The Bank Dick," should be required viewing for every student of humor.

As one who had "The Bank Dick" memorized years ago, while it was still being revived in movie houses, I resent every second that has been pruned out of it for TV pur-poses. But it is only in classics that I mind this cutting. Otherwise it is a positive virtue. It gives the old movie fan still another game, one that no other form of drama offers. This is the game of guessing what has been snipped from the original and, consequently, what the movie can possibly be about.

The plot yawns with huge gaps. A scene will end with a man and woman happily married. Three minutes and five commercials later, when the film resumes, the couple will be long divorced and married to new partners. I have left men in New York and, after the commercial, found them for no conceivable reason in Macao or Tangier. I have pieced together, after the fact, hundreds of births, deaths, triumphs, failures, fights, reconciliations and other pivotal events.

It is always exciting to pick up the scent again and again, despite the cutter's best efforts to throw me off. Thus to my movie-watching pleasures two final treats are added. One is suspense: the breathless waiting to see not simply "how it will come out," but whether it will come out. The other is the satisfaction of solving a puzzle that has undoubtedly stumped thousands of viewers across America.

Obviously my addiction is so severe that I am beyond medical help. No wonder I silently pray, as every old film crackles to its end, that the next thing I hear will be the "Star-Spangled Banner" and not the voice of the announcer saying "And now for the late, late, *late* movie!"

20. "Will Nobody Bid Any More?"

IN THE HIGHLY COMPETITIVE GAME OF acquiring status, nothing gives the American player so many points right now as the ownership of fine art. The process of collecting, however, does not get its real start in America. It takes most of its direction and impetus from the London auction firm of Sotheby & Co., which has jumped to fame and wealth lately with its spectacular sales of paintings and antiques. In the operation of this one firm the whole remarkable boom can be traced.

Perhaps the most dazzling gift shared by the nine men and one woman who own and manage Sotheby's is the

ability to know a valuable object when they see one—
even if they have never seen such an object before. Typical
of their art and scholarship, and of the route by which
most items reach the firm, was an incident that took place
not long ago. A man brought in a curious round instrument, only three inches in diameter, that he had found in
a second-hand shop. It was immediately taken, as all incoming objects are, to the appropriate Sotheby expert—
in this case, T. H. Clarke, who heads the department called
"objects of art."

Unlike the tidy realms that his colleagues supervise, such
as silver or furniture or books, "objects of art" is a vague
domain bounded on all sides by avid collectors and filled
with strange and wonderful things: icons and miniatures,
snuffboxes and glass paperweights, clocks and rings and, as
Mr. Clarke puts it, "everything that isn't everything else."
He so expects the unexpected to turn up on his desk every
morning that he is never surprised when it does.

Still, the instrument that turned up on this particular
morning was more than ordinarily unexpected, for nothing
of its type had previously appeared. (Sotheby directors also
seem to have total recall.) From its Islamic metalwork and
Arabic script Mr. Clarke dated it to the Middle Ages and
suspected its importance. To identify it more exactly he
telephoned a science scholar and described the odd little
globe.

"What you are describing," the scholar said, "is a spheri-
cal astrolabe, but I must warn you that it doesn't exist.
We know from medieval manuscripts that it *did* exist, but
nobody has ever found one." Obviously, however, somebody had found one. The unique object, lost for 500 years
and still guarding the secret of how it got to London, became the central jewel in an auction of instruments that
Mr. Clarke was arranging, where it attracted lively interest
and "fetched" $10,000.

To think of Sotheby's in these terms—as a contest that any amateur can enter—does not occur to a reader of newspapers. Judging by the glamorous auctions that the company holds so often and with such fanfare, it would seem to be a business only for art dealers and millionaires. Yet the firm's success actually rests on the hundreds of smaller sales that it holds all year long, day in and day out. Its annual gross now approaches $30,000,000—more than the combined income of its three principal rivals, Christie's of London, Parke-Bernet of New York and the Galérie Charpentier of Paris—but this money does not come mainly from paintings or from a rich clientele. Two thousand people a day wander through the Sotheby building on New Bond Street; half the objects that they buy there cost less than $75, and only a small proportion of them are paintings.

It is this perpetual traffic with all sorts of people and all sorts of possessions that makes Sotheby's such a lively marketplace—and one so rich in surprises. No week elapses when somebody does not discover in his home an unremembered and unloved object whose value has risen to thousands of dollars. Generally he has no idea how steep the rise has been, and has been using his uncommon trophy for the commonest purpose. Several years ago, after a Benin bronze was auctioned at Sotheby's for almost $8,000, two more of these extremely rare Nigerian heads were brought in by owners who saw newspaper accounts of the sale.

One head had long served as a doorstop. The other had been repeatedly polished to a shiny yellow, like any household trinket, and so had lost all of its patina and much of its value. Nevertheless such events always stir a double sense of adventure at Sotheby's. The collector is thrilled by the appearance of a rarity that was not known to exist, and the seller is equally thrilled by the sum that the unwanted heirloom brings. It is one modern equivalent of finding buried treasure.

With such a vast daily turnover Sotheby's has become more than just a marketplace. It is a business giant which exerts power in many directions. The financial community watches it as an index to the economy; artists, designers and dealers watch it as a weathervane that tells where the winds of taste are blowing. Almost nowhere are new currents so quickly felt. The objects that Sotheby's handles, after all, represent 5,000 years of man's efforts to create beauty and every bizarre turn that his mind has taken in this pursuit. Thus the firm is in a position to satisfy the most finicky customer.

For the mind of the collector has been, if anything, even more bizarre than that of the artist. This strange bird, so given to unpredictable swoops, is the real center of the auction business, and the story of Sotheby's is largely the story of its ability to cater to the bird's fickle appetites. Who would expect anyone to pay, as a collector recently did, $3,500 for a glass paperweight of a snake swallowing a fly?

In this story there is as much for the social historian as for the art historian to ponder. For never have so many people in so many countries been on such an art-buying spree, and never has the urge been so intertwined with factors that have nothing to do with art. Many of these factors are economic (art is a good investment and a tax benefit). Many are rooted in snobbery (art is the new status symbol). Some have their origin in modern architecture (people who live in glass houses can't have Grand Rapids furniture and "September Morn"). Some can be traced to that canny puppeteer, the interior decorator, who decrees from season to season which King George is in (III) and which is out (IV).

But whatever the motives, the result is the same. Art

and antique prices continue their upward arc, and Sotheby directors see no end to the curve, for the number of collectors is multiplying and the number of fine objects is not. In fact, it is shrinking. For dozens of new museums are being born, especially in the United States, and each must have its Picasso, its Queen Anne silver, Chippendale chair, Ming vase and Egyptian head. When these objects lodge in a museum they go out of circulation, and the remaining objects in individual homes become that much rarer. Privately the directors of Sotheby's say that the current prices are "fantastic" and "ridiculous." But there is nothing ridiculous about their position as middlemen in the art stampede.

For a business so centrally fixed, Sotheby's is easy to miss on a stroll up New Bond Street. The old three-story building tends to disappear amid the other gilded shops, possibly because its façade is bisected by a newsstand. Like many English houses of a certain age, it derives part of its charm from not being entirely plumb. Perhaps it has been tilted by the hordes of pilgrims who swarm in every morning in search of a bargain, a good browse or simply an entertaining show.

The show begins—in fact, the whole operation begins—downstairs at the counter where people bring the objects that they want to put up for auction. To watch this parade of odd-shaped bundles is to see how deeply the magpie instinct has taken hold in the human race. Old ladies rummage about in bulky reticules and fish out silver tea services. Brown paper bags disgorge faïence dishes in grotesque animal and vegetable form. A Mayfair lady will stride in bearing a half-dozen sconces; another will be followed by her chauffeur carrying a mosaic table-top. Bearded Bohemians arrive with abstract paintings, bookish men with first editions and musty prints, dowagers with rolled-up rugs and Oriental pillows, and soon the counter is piled as high as a stall in an Arab bazaar, the objects having no common thread except that they are no longer wanted at home.

The girls behind the counter, increasingly harried as the morning races on, take the objects to a Sotheby director, or call one out to meet the object and its owner. This process is rather like a doctor's examination: the object is poked and inspected while its parent stands nervously by. Frequently the verdict is disappointing:

"I'm afraid it *isn't* Queen Anne, Madam—much nearer Queen Victoria, unfortunately."

"It really isn't rare at all, sir, I'm sorry to say, no matter what your grandmother told you. I doubt it would fetch three pounds."

"I must tell you that it isn't genuine. Mind you, it's a very *clever* fake, but we've seen several of these lately."

Back go the objects into the reticules and brown paper bags, unworthy of auction. If the verdict is favorable—that is, if the object has a certain market value—Sothebys will estimate what it will fetch, and the owner will name a "reserve" price below which the auctioneer must not sell. So giddy is today's market, spurting up visibly from month to month, that these estimates can be far off. Not long ago a lady from Australia brought in a small James I wine cup (*c.* 1607) that she had never thought much of—she kept her car keys in it. The Sotheby man, struck by its grace and lineage, felt that it might fetch $2,000. The lady, eager to be rid of it, fixed the reserve at $900, and the cup actually went for $3,400.

"It even surprised us," one director said, "and we're supposed to be experts." This phrase is heard often in Sotheby's nowadays, proving that the auction business is a game of chance that the auctioneer himself can never wholly control. He has no way of knowing what people will turn up at an auction or what instructions bring them there. He cannot foresee the whims and passions that goad two collectors to bid against each other, long after cooler heads have quit the field, for an object that only one of them can own. Nor can he predict the occasional moment when this process reverses itself, unaccountably, and all bidding stops far below the expected figure.

Every auction begins, in a sense, several weeks in advance when a catalogue is mailed out to subscribers all over the world. In this deceptively simple booklet they can read an account of each item and decide whether to bid and how —in person, by mail or through a dealer. (Auction firms tend to rise or fall on the reliability of their catalogues; the Sotheby staff prides itself on the scholarship of these books.) The customer's decision often hinges on how he deciphers the catalogue's special codes, particularly the one whereby Sotheby's declares a work to be authentic, possibly authentic or probably not. The key to this code is the fullness of the artist's name. Thus a painting by "Sir Anthony Van Dyck" is genuine (one of these recently went for $11,200) and a painting by "A. Van Dyck" is dubious (one of these went at the same auction for $785). Any further bobbing of the name would suggest that V. Dyck almost surely didn't get near the canvas.

The auction itself is, of course, the main event of any day at Sotheby's. One is held every morning from eleven to one in the gallery on the second floor—a long green room with skylights that let in large amounts of sun and small amounts of rain—and often a book auction proceeds simultaneously in an adjoining room. The selling of books was the chief business of Sotheby's from its founding in 1744 until well into the twentieth century, when the art boom gathered momentum, and the ritual appears to have changed little in the 200-odd years since. Several dozen book dealers sit gravely in a circle beneath the auctioneer, who nods from side to side to accept their barely perceptible bids. This is an arena for experts: knowledge is precise, emotions are neat, and long tradition lends its august presence.

By contrast, the main gallery is a carnival where any fool can try his luck. At first it fills the visitor with awe. In the spiraling zeros of the auctioneer's voice—"two thousand pounds, two thousand five *hun*dred, *three* thousand pounds"—the private wealth of modern man seems limitless and overwhelming. But after several visits the room assumes its proper size and loses its goblins. The people are seen to be merely people, the objects shed their sanctity and are seen to be merely beautiful objects that anybody might have inherited or might aspire to buy. Often, in fact, they seem to be going at such a bargain rate that the visitor is tempted to jump into the bidding himself. Meanwhile he tries hard to keep his hand from wandering, frozen by the ancient fear that if he scratches his head he will acquire a Renoir. This danger is overestimated. Auctioneers can tell when a lady is bidding and when she is waving to a friend, even if the friend can't, and if in doubt they will ask.

Of the hundreds of people who attend every auction, relatively few are obvious dealers. They sit at a green baize table in front of the auctioneer with casual authority verging on boredom. The rest of the spectators drift in and out while the auction is in progress, greeting their friends, chatting, making notes, listening with half an ear, watching with half an eye and, at sporadic moments, wagging their catalogue to bid. So informal is the coming and going that the affair is very much like a large cocktail party. Presumably many Londoners make a habit of dropping in, during their morning rounds, to keep in touch with the market and with each other.

As a crowd they do not have, as might be expected, a common gold link. The aristocracy turns up in sufficient number to prove that the monocle, the eye-level bowler and the walking stick are not figments of "Punch" cartoonists and English film-makers. But the Mayfair set has no majority in the saleroom. Disheveled young artists, looking quite penniless, will suddenly bid on a painting—perhaps an earlier work of their own or of a still-"undiscovered" friend. Mothers will stop in for a while with young children to give them a taste of beauty. Old men who have been attending auctions for fifty years will sit and exchange saleroom gossip until the one obscure item that interests them—antique firearms, possibly, or horse trappings—comes up for sale. American collectors, over on the night plane to get a specific object, will get it and leave to catch the afternoon flight back. Sleek dealers from the continent in pinched suits and pointed shoes, buying for the *"Dolce Vita"* crowd at home, mingle the languages of Italy, France, Germany and other lands into the English brew—proof of how widely the items assembled for this auction will soon be scattered again.

The objects themselves are not, as in many auction houses, kept aloof from the customers and brought out at the moment of sale to be displayed from a stage. On the contrary, a visitor at an auction today may well sit on a Heppelwhite fourposter that is coming up for sale tomorrow, or stand on a valuable rug that will be sold out from under him that very morning. The glittering chandeliers overhead and the Flemish tapestries on the walls, which seem to be part of the permanent decor on Monday, will be gone by Friday and replaced by something else.

A similar hodgepodge fills the three small surrounding

rooms. These objects, on view for several days before they come up for auction, are also perfectly approachable, and browsers spend many hours there fondling silver, examining porcelain and jewelry, and riffling through prints. A ladder is available for those who want an intimate look at the paintings, and it is not uncommon to see an old gentleman, beyond the age of exercise by ordinary standards, lug the ladder from one room to another, climb up it and peer at an Old Master, or pseudo-Old Master, through a magnifying glass.

In this atmosphere of calculated clutter—Sotheby's has somehow turned to picturesque advantage the fact that its building is too small—a visitor is beguiled into thinking that the ill-assorted objects will never be sorted out again. In the apparent disorder, however, there is always order. Beneath its quaint veneer the firm rests on a solid base of artistic knowledge, business shrewdness and human intuition.

For these three traits to exist in equal balance in one business is rare enough. That they should exist in one man is rarer still, and as this man is chairman of Sotheby's he represents the ideal conjunction of man and job. In his ten years as boss Peter Wilson has tripled the company's business and has been the chief architect of its rise. Now fifty-two, he bestrides the world art market like a colossus, or, more properly, like a sphinx, for in his cherubic face there is always the half-smile that hints of happy endings for everybody, of beautiful mysteries that only he can translate.

This mixture of charm and self-assurance has also become, by reflection, the personality of Sotheby's as a whole. "Before the war," says Mr. Wilson, who joined the firm at twenty-four and became a director at twenty-six, "the atmosphere was more formal. I've tried to make it more

easygoing. I want people to feel at home, whether they're
here for any serious purpose or not. If you threw out 90
percent of the visitors because they didn't come to bid,
the sale would go less well. They contribute to the
atmosphere."

Wilson's own personality is most potently on display
when he "takes a sale." A very tall, rosy, blue-eyed man,
whose accent purrs with the cadences of Eton, Oxford and
all else that is Established in the British order, whose
striped pants and morning coat evoke the highest spheres of
diplomacy, he looms out of the auctioneer's pulpit like a
benign prime minister who has never lost a vote of con-
fidence—and never expects to. His voice can register shades
of meaning so subtle that the human ear barely catches
them. When he says, after the bidding has soared to a vast
sum and suddenly come to a halt, "Three thousand pounds,
then," or "Three thousand only," there is just enough
extra weight on "then" or "only" to convey a tinge of
disappointment, almost of disbelief, that an object of such
value should be going for so little. Quite often this nudges
the bidders back into action and they drive the price up
still higher.

Wilson's most shameless performance took place six
years ago at the Jakob Goldschmidt auction, where seven
Impressionist paintings went for $2,186,800. This was the
first of the fabulous auctions of the postwar era and the
one that announced the arrival of Sotheby's at the top of
the heap. So huge were the prices, by 1958 standards, as
the sale proceeded—a Van Gogh fetched $369,000, a Manet
$316,400—that the spectators were tense when Cézanne's
"Boy in a Red Waistcoat" came up.

Bidding soon reached the unprecedented figure of $616,-
000 and then paused. In the ensuing silence Wilson said,
"Will nobody bid any more?" The outrageous remark, so

casually delivered, broke the room into laughter and broke
the tension for good. Nobody *did* bid any more, and Wilson
is not sure to this day if he didn't abridge the sale. If so, he
isn't worrying about it. He recalls the moment with vast
amusement. "It was absolutely idiotic," he says, giggling
with delight.

Since then Wilson has captured many other brilliant
auctions for Sotheby's—he has a way of turning up in
Pittsburgh, say, or Milan just when a collector is "ready
to talk," and he would be a hard man *not* to entrust with
a sale. His charm is one of the firm's most negotiable assets,
and it is reinforced by an aesthetic judgment and commercial sense that his colleagues regard as infallible. Today
the big auctions that he conducts are social events of the
London scene—a fact demonstrated almost too well by
the sale of Somerset Maugham's paintings on April 9, 1962.
There Sotheby's fully learned the extent to which it has
become the victim of its own strenuous publicity.

Into the protesting old building, at 9:30 P.M., pushed
2,500 people, or roughly a thousand more than could com-
fortably fit, and hundreds more were turned away. A large
number were titled, moneyed or vested with power; the
remainder were vested with curiosity, and thus the event
took on the aura of a Hollywood premiere. A long platform
sagged under newsreel and TV cameras, which whirred so
noisily that they often drowned out the bidders. Roving
photographers shoved through the elegant crowd to snap
such arriving mandarins as Lord Beaverbrook, and a nurse
waited with great solemnity to revive the faint.

Under all this bodily pressure the renowned English
calm buckled. Spectators jostled for position and took their
losses badly. "Thank God at least we're in England," one
old gentleman said, "and not in Italy: a charming people
but very excitable." Those who couldn't squeeze into the

main gallery were hurled back into various surrounding rooms, where they watched the auction on TV and had their bids relayed by phone to the auctioneer. This, needless to say, was Peter Wilson, collating the different bids and tranquillizing the nervous throng. Within an hour he disposed of Maugham's thirty-five unexceptional paintings for almost $1,500,000, the highest price being $224,000 for a two-sided work by Picasso, and retired secure in the knowledge that the sale would make the front page of the "New York Times" the next day.

The firm would also be richer by $150,000. Its standard commission is 10 percent, or considerably less than that of its competitors in other countries, such as Parke-Bernet, which charges 20 percent. As a result, countless Americans now send their objects abroad to be auctioned at Sotheby's. Since these objects are frequently bought by other Americans, it is common for paintings or pieces of furniture to cross the ocean, change ownership and take one of the next boats back.

The visible drama of the Sotheby auction room is the final product of much invisible machinery, run by ten partners who share the profits and pleasures of the business. Each is an expert in one field and often in many more, as, for example, J. C. Butterwick is an authority on books and silver, and A. J. B. Kiddell, a specialist in porcelain, is consulted by his colleagues on almost any baffling object that strays into the house.

In this respect, and because each man runs his own department independently, Sotheby's resembles a small college, whose professors are bound in a fellowship of learning and taste. They work hard, at tasks that are essentially academic: selecting, evaluating and cataloguing the objects that they will subsequently auction, and at the same time teaching their junior assistants ("What's the one thing wrong with that vase?"). They occupy cramped offices that can hardly be reached because the aisles are clogged with objects awaiting auction, especially in the vaulted cellar where 3,000 paintings are often stacked, and they sit at desks littered with treasures awaiting their scrutiny. Their phone rings and their door opens constantly to admit some question that needs an immediate answer or to inform them that they must fly to Madrid right away to appraise a collection. Harried by detail, they still—like professors—do not regard what they do as work. It is a game that never fails to divert.

"We just sit here like Micawber waiting for things to turn up," says R. S. Timewell, head of the furniture department. "Recently an old lady near Cambridge wrote that she wanted to raise $5,500 and asked if I would go through her house and see if her furniture would fetch that much. I did, and there was absolutely nothing of value. As I was about to leave I said, 'Have I seen *every-thing*?' She said I had, except for a maid's room that she hadn't bothered to show me. The room turned out to have a very fine eighteenth-century chest that the old lady was using to store blankets in. 'Your worries are over,' I told her, 'if you sell that chest.' She said, 'But that's quite impossible—where will I store my blankets?'

"I told her that she could buy a new chest for about $25 and store her blankets in that. She said, 'That sounds a good idea.' The chest was auctioned for $6,500 and is now a prize piece in an American home."

Sometimes this happens on a scale so big as to sound like romantic fiction. "Several years ago a Captain Berkeley wrote us," recalls Frederick Rose, director of the silver department, "and said that he had a silver dinner service for which someone had offered him $140,000, and he wondered if he should accept the offer. I didn't know of this particular service, nor, it seems, did anybody else. I went out to Berkeley Castle to see it, and it turned out to be a 168-piece Louis XV service by Jacques Roettiers, one of only three to survive the French Revolution.

"I felt that it would fetch a much higher price if it were put up to public competition. The question was whether to sell it as a unit or break it up. We were strongly advised to break it up, but we thought that would be terrible, so we decided to sell it *in toto*. On the day of the auction Captain Berkeley came and said he hoped we had made the right decision. Well, the opening bid was $140,-000—it was from the same man who had made the original offer—and after that the bidding went up in multiples of five thousand pounds. It was all over in two minutes: the service sold for $579,600. And Captain Berkeley himself only had it insured for $8,000. That was part of the charm of the whole thing."

It may seem inconceivable that such a treasure could remain a secret in a nation where almost nothing has gone unrecorded since 1066. Yet the great houses of England are only beginning to yield their ancestral treasures. This is especially true of paintings, according to Carmen Gronau, the firm's expert on Old Masters and its only woman director. "There's an enormous fund of pictures in England," says Mrs. Gronau, "that is unlike anything else in the world. Great paintings are apt to turn up from the most unexpected sources, or even medium paintings. A winter landscape by Jan Van Goyen went recently for $19,-000; it belonged to an almost impoverished woman who had inherited it.

"The wealth of this country came in the eighteenth and nineteenth centuries, when the sons went on the grand tour and bought paintings. The large collections are all known—the big houses of the nobility in England are like the small princely houses of Europe—but the bread and butter comes from the broad general fund, from what the trade calls 'a good country source,' which is something that comes fresh on the market. The owners of these works have always just had them on the wall and taken them for granted—until now. When Franz Hals' 'Portrait of a Cavalier' came to us for auction four years ago—it sold for $509,000—it was almost completely unknown. It had only been exhibited once, in 1922, in a provincial museum."

Equally hidden from the public all these years was Rembrandt's "Saint Bartholomew," which Major Kincaid Lennox sold at Sotheby's two years ago for $532,000. Major Lennox seldom admits people who want to see his inherited collection, which includes two other Rembrandts and a Van Dyck, and which shares a room in his Shropshire castle with a television set and a budgie. When these little-known works will seep out on the market, and how many other English houses contain such unseen masterpieces, is anybody's guess, though the Treasury Department probably has a pretty good one.

It is the need for money, after all—especially money to meet huge death duties and other taxes—that is dislodging the great hoards of art, silver, furniture, jewelry and books from the stately homes of Albion. Those who listen closely at Sotheby's can hear more than the crack of the auctioneer's gavel. They can hear the cracking of ancient estates, the tottering of peerages and, in the distance, the onrush of the new rich—Englishmen who made postwar fortunes in scrap or realty, Greek shipping magnates, Italian and German industrialists, American oil tycoons and other first-generation millionaires, all eager for the attributes of status and taste that can be had at Sotheby's for the raising of a hand and the writing of a check.

"Today it has become almost essential, if one's income is over a certain amount, to furnish one's house with antique things," says Mr. Timewell, who has seen furniture prices soar so high that a collector recently paid $92,400 for a Louis XV commode. "On the whole, people don't buy an object here because they're astonished by its rarity, or interested in its history, but because it's authentic. Antique furniture is a symbol of prestige and a sound investment; new furniture can cost just as much, and it has no resale value.

"The demand for fine objects is so great that people will buy almost anything, regardless of whether it's in fashion. Not Americans, though. When a style goes out of vogue in the United States, nobody there will buy it. English people don't know it's out of vogue in the United States, and if you told them it would be the least of their worries. The English are more conservative and not so swayed by fads. Americans are very susceptible to the advice of decorators.

"I gather that tapestries, for example, are unsalable in America today. But Italian, Dutch, German and English buyers are very keen on them. They were great status symbols in the seventeenth and eighteenth centuries—they cost immense amounts then, probably ten times what they would fetch today. American tourists bought them in great volume in Europe around 1900, but their children rolled them up and put them in warehouses and are now selling them off here."

The tapestries are only one proof of the fact that in today's art market almost nothing is a dud. Every department head at Sotheby's, surveying his field, bears this out. In silver, for instance, it is generally assumed that "you can double or even triple your money in five years."

"All fine books have appreciated in value," says A. R. A. Hobson, head of the book department, "and medieval manuscripts also keep rising. In 1900 Sotheby's sold an eleventh-century manuscript of Boethius for $100; a few years ago it came through again and fetched $18,000." In 1960 Mr. Hobson concluded an auction of manuscripts collected by C. W. Dyson Perrins which brought almost two and a half million dollars. He has also presided over the gradual sale of three private libraries—libraries so big that they took eight, ten and sixteen years, respectively, to auction off. Annual sales of books at Sotheby's now total roughly $3,000,000.

In antique furniture only two styles, according to Mr. Timewell, are "relatively out of vogue: very elaborately carved furniture of about 1800, and Renaissance furniture, which was tremendously high at the turn of this century and can be bought for little today. "Modern art is booming —and breeding a whole new race of British art lovers, according to R. J. Rickett, the firm's expert in everything less old than an Old Master. "Up to now," he says, "hunting, shooting and fishing have been the occupational pastimes in England, and the pictures on English walls were faded aquatints of Midlands steeplechases. Anyone who collected modern art was considered Bohemian or a very queer fellow."

In the catch-all realm of *"vertu,"* miniatures are one of the few items where the supply exceeds the demand, and even this gap is closing fast. Otherwise this realm consists of all sorts of oddities, such as glass paperweights, which have been made both scarce and expensive by zealous collectors. (Several years ago Sotheby's sold 800 paperweights for $18,000.) Porcelain and china figures are in enormous demand, and still in fairly big supply, as opposed to Oriental pottery, which is far rarer and intensely sought after.

"There are nowhere near enough early Chinese ceramics

to go around," Mr. Kiddell points out. "It's mostly stuff that circulates through private collections in Europe, since nothing comes out of China itself. Prices have literally shot up. The keenest demand is for blue and white wares of the Yuan and early Ming period. Those are really the primitives of Chinese porcelain.

"I remember several years ago a teen-age boy came in with a fifteenth-century blue and white dish. He had bought it in a junk shop in the East End for $15 because he thought it looked valuable, and it was—it sold for $7,000. That shows it can still be done if you're alert. But it's getting harder. Everyone knows his porcelain better now, so the real finds will have to be made in minor arts that are not as widely written about, like early Ming lacquer and cloisonné But books are beginning to come out on these subjects, too, and they will raise the general level of awareness."

This is a point that all the Sotheby directors make in accounting for the boom in their business. Art books, films, museums, house tours and other media have spread art knowledge on a broad popular base, and even the most esoteric fields are no longer the province of the scholarly few. Inevitably this has increased the desire to own fine objects and is driving collectors to find new fields to collect. Their restless search is felt at Sotheby's mainly in the antiquities department, which, despite its name, ranges from the oldest classical civilizations to the primitive art of modern man.

By now, of course, the great antiquities have been put into museums and out of reach. Quite a few countries have also adopted stern rules—notably Egypt, Greece, Italy, India and Nigeria—to keep their national treasures from leaving the country. Yet certain obscure art forms keep turning up to pique the collector's fancy. One is "Roman glass," a name given to the iridescent vials and scent bottles of the Roman Empire. These objects have jumped into popular demand in the past few years. So have pre-Columbian gold ornaments, Etruscan statues and Cycladic Greek figures. Haida objects are also catching on; these are small bone and ivory carvings of the Haida tribe in British Columbia.

"Of course nobody really knows," says Mr. Clarke, speaking of the whole inflated market, "what any of the objects that come up for auction today are worth. If they did, there wouldn't be any auction business."

"You must deal with every sale as a special problem, not by an established system," says Peter Wilson. "It is an art, not a science." Under his leadership Sotheby's has learned to practice this art with near-scientific precision. Yet he knows that the current boom can be explained only up to a point in terms of snobbery, tax laws, investments, publicity, education and other such factors. Far more subtle forces are at work which unbalance the formula, adding new elements of mystery and surprise.

"For many people," Wilson says, "buying a fine object is, in a sense, buying a stake in the future. It takes the place of religion, especially in insecure times. It's like old people planting trees. A gentleman of eighty thinks nothing of planting a forest of trees. After the war, the first items to rise dramatically in price were porcelains, the most fragile of all. If you buy a very fragile object, or a very rare or beautiful object, you are saying that life is going to go on."

About the Author

William K. Zinsser was for many years a critic and editorial writer for the New York *Herald Tribune*. A free-lance since 1959, his articles appear in *Life, The Saturday Evening Post, Horizon, Esquire* and other magazines.

His books include *Any Old Place With You, Seen Any Good Movies Lately?, The City Dwellers* and *Weekend Guests*. He is also co-author (with Howard Lindsay, Harry Golden, Walt Kelly and John Updike) of *Five Boyhoods*.

Mr. Zinsser is entertainment critic of the NBC-TV "Sunday" program.

He has written the music and lyrics of an original musical comedy, with book by James Stevenson, that is scheduled for production this fall.

He lives in New York City with his wife and two children, Amy and John William.

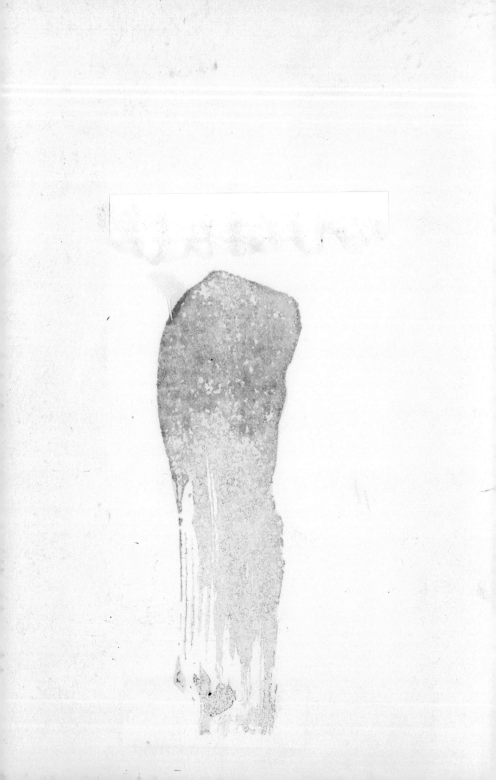